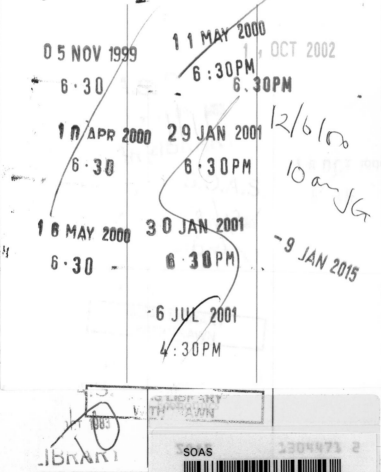

THE ECONOMICS OF THE
DEVELOPING COUNTRIES

H. Myint

Professor of Economics in the London School of
Economics and Political Science

HUTCHINSON

London Melbourne Sydney Auckland Johannesburg

Hutchinson & Co. (Publishers) Ltd

An imprint of the Hutchinson Publishing Group

17–21 Conway Street, London WIP 6JD

Hutchinson Group (Australia) Pty Ltd
30–32 Cremorne Street, Richmond South, Victoria 3121
PO Box 151, Broadway, New South Wales 2007

Hutchinson Group (NZ) Ltd
32–34 View Road, PO Box 40–086, Glenfield, Auckland 10

Hutchinson Group (SA) (Pty) Ltd
PO Box 337, Bergvlei 2012, South Africa

First published 1964
Reprinted 1964
Second edition 1965
Third edition 1967
Reprinted 1969
Fourth edition 1973
Reprinted 1974, 1977
Fifth edition 1980
Reprinted 1980, 1982

Printed in Great Britain by The Anchor Press Ltd
and bound by Wm Brendon & Son Ltd
both of Tiptree, Essex

British Library Cataloguing in Publication Data

Myint, Hla
Economics of the developing countries. – 5th ed.
1. Underdeveloped areas – Economic conditions
I. Title
330.9′172′4   HC59.7

ISBN 0 09 140241 7

CONTENTS

I

INTRODUCTION:

THE POST-WAR APPROACH TO

THE UNDERDEVELOPED COUNTRIES

There are two main driving forces behind the study of the under-developed countries. The first, which has grown rapidly under the pressure of post-war international tensions, is concerned with the need to do something urgently about the problem of poverty in these countries. The second, which has a longer academic tradition, is concerned with trying to understand the reasons for the great differences in economic development between the underdeveloped and the developed countries; it is concerned with the nature and causes of the 'Poverty of Nations'. Current ideas of the under-developed countries can best be understood against the background of these two approaches and their interaction upon each other.

The first line of approach focuses attention on the large difference in the per capita national income levels between the developed and the underdeveloped countries. This difference is regarded as the measure of the gap in the standards of living among the rich and the poor countries, highlighting the *prima facie* case for the rich to help the poor. Further, it is argued that the low level of per capita incomes of the underdeveloped countries is a major cause of their slow rate of growth and economic stagnation. These countries are said to be trapped in a 'vicious circle' of poverty, aggravated by growing population pressure on limited land: low incomes leading to a low level of saving and investment, leading to low productivity of labour and low incomes. It is (or used to be) maintained that the 'vicious circle' can be broken only by a 'crash' programme of econo-mic development requiring a large inflow of international aid to supplement the inadequate domestic saving of the underdeveloped countries.

Now, one can readily accept the broad fact that the underdeveloped countries typically have a much lower level of material standard of living than the developed countries. But there is a considerable margin of error and ambiguity in trying to measure the gap in the standards of living from the different levels of per capita national incomes.

To begin with, the standard of living of a country depends, not on its per capita income as such, but on its per capita consumption. But in the poorer underdeveloped countries, the dividing line between 'consumption' and 'investment' is blurred. For instance, consumption expenditure which increases the nutrition and improves the health and productive efficiency of the people can claim to be regarded as 'investment' as much as the installation of a new machine. On the other hand, some underdeveloped countries attempt to pursue drastic methods of mobilizing savings and cutting down present consumption for the sake of accelerating future economic growth. In such a context, the distinction between per capita consumption and per capita income may be important. Next, the poverty of a country is more accurately reflected by the representative standard of living among the great mass of its population than by its per capita income. This representative income may be well below the average obtained by dividing the total national income of a country by its total population when income is unequally distributed. This consideration, ignored during the 1950s,[1] has come back to the forefront in recent times and will be considered later.

Then there are a number of well-known difficulties which arise in trying to compare the real income levels of different countries on the basis of the differences in money income levels. We may mention three of them.

First, we shall have to make allowances for the obvious but quantitatively important differences in the requirements for food, clothing, heating and shelter in different climates; most of the under-developed countries are in the tropics while most of the developed countries are in the temperate zone.

Second, we shall have to take into account the differences in the general stage of economic development, specifically, the degree of development of the exchange economy among the countries compared. A substantial part of the national product of the underdeveloped countries still takes the form of 'subsistence production' of food and other consumers' goods by small peasant farmers and their families

[1] cf. J. Viner, *International Trade and Economic Development*, The Clarendon Press, Oxford 1953, pp. 99–100.

for their own consumption. Although this subsistence output is not bought and sold, its imputed cash value has to be included in the national incomes of the underdeveloped countries to make them comparable with the national incomes of other countries where the exchange economy is more fully developed. There is a considerable margin of error both in estimating the physical quantities of subsistence output and in selecting appropriate accounting prices to value the different constituents of subsistence output. Further, the subsistence sector tends to shrink over time with the spread of exchange economy in the course of economic development. In this process, the goods which were previously freely obtainable through fishing, hunting or the gathering of forest produce would have to be purchased with money. Thus the growth of money incomes in a developing country is partly made up of the monetization of subsistence activity without a genuine increase in the physical quantity of goods and services available for consumption. Turning to the other side of the comparison, there is an important qualification to be introduced in interpreting the high levels of money incomes in the highly urbanized industrial countries. The real income level tends to be overestimated by the inclusion of a great number of 'cost' items, such as the cost of daily travel to work or the cost of reducing industrial pollution as items of income.

Third, international comparisons of incomes involve computing the national incomes of the individual countries in their own currencies and then converting the resultant figures into a common denominator, viz. the US dollar at the official exchange rates. An important source of error can arise from the choice of the exchange rate. Usually, the appropriateness of the exchange rate of a country is considered from the standpoint of maintaining its balance of payments equilibrium. Thus many underdeveloped countries, which have fixed their exchange rate at a level which does not adequately reflect their higher domestic rate of inflation relative to the general international rate of inflation, tend to get into balance of payments difficulties because of their 'overvalued' currency. Conversion of their national incomes at these 'overvalued' exchange rates will overestimate their real incomes relative to those of countries with a more moderate rate of inflation. But as against this, there is another factor which leads to an underestimation of the real incomes of the poorer underdeveloped countries relative to the advanced countries, even when the exchange rates are appropriate for the purpose of maintaining the balance of payments equilibrium. This arises from the existence of the 'domestic' goods and services which do not enter into international trade; or more precisely, from the different proportions in which the national output of the underdeveloped countries enter into international trade.   In the advanced countries with a higher degree of internal economic development, the costs and prices of the non-traded 'domestic' goods are closely related to the higher wages and productivity of labour in the export industries.   In contrast, the prices of the 'domestic' goods and services in the underdeveloped countries tend to reflect the general low levels of income and earnings of the local labour rather than the higher wages and productivity of labour in their export industries or their urban manufacturing industries producing import substitutes.   For this reason, the 'domestic' goods and services of the underdeveloped countries are likely to be underestimated when valued at the official exchange rates.   These exchange rates even when appropriate for the internationally traded goods do not really reflect the purchasing power of the currencies over the domestic goods and tend to exaggerate the differences in labour productivity in the 'domestic' goods sectors of the developed and the underdeveloped countries.   Thus the poorer an underdeveloped country or the lower the ratio of its national output entering into international trade, the more its real income is likely to be underestimated relative to its nominal income at the official exchange rate.   This source of underestimation is likely to be greatest for a country like India which has both a relatively low level of income and low ratio of international trade to total income because of its size.[1]

Apart from these qualifications, the per capita national income approach to the underdeveloped countries, which once dominated thinking has been put under an increasing strain from a more obvious cause: the per capita incomes of these countries as conventionally calculated have grown more rapidly than was ever dreamt of in the 1950s.   During that period, the typical per capita income of the underdeveloped countries was considered to be about $100 or less a year (in terms of the current purchasing power of the US dollar at that time) contrasted with the per capita income of $1000 or more a year for the developed countries.   The dividing line between the two groups of countries was then drawn at $400 with some special cases such as an underdeveloped country like Argentina having an income above that level and an industrialized country like Japan having an

[1] cf. I. B. Kravis, A. W. Heston and R. Summers, 'Real GDP *per capita* for more than one hundred countries', *Economic Journal*, June 1978.

income a little below that level.   By the 1960s, the average per capita income for the underdeveloped countries as a group was estimated to have risen to about $200 a year, with a range of $100 to $500. The per capita income for the developed countries, including Japan, ranged between $1500 and over $4000 a year.   Since then, all these figures have been continually revised upwards.   Recently, the World Bank has abandoned the traditional practice of giving an overall average per capita income figure for the underdeveloped countries as a group.   In its *World Development Report 1978*, the ninety-two developing countries are now reclassified into thirty-four 'Low Income Countries' and fifty-eight 'Middle Income Countries'.   The 'Low Income Countries' have an average per capita income of $150 (in terms of the 1976 US dollar) and the 'Middle Income Countries' have an average income of $750.   But the income range for the latter group is very wide, extending from $250 to $3000.   The average per capita income for the developed 'Industrialized Countries' is $6200 but there is an overlap in the incomes between the richer 'Middle Income Countries' such as Singapore and Venezuela with the poorer 'Industrialized Countries' such as South Africa and Ireland.   The oil-rich Middle East countries have higher per capita incomes than the 'Industrialized Countries', with Kuwait having the world's highest per capita income of $15,480 a year.[1]

Let us now turn from the level to the rate of growth of per capita incomes among the underdeveloped countries.   The fact that their average per capita incomes appeared to have risen during the 1950–60 decade was properly treated with caution.   But when the upward trend continued during the 1960–70 decade, it began to be accepted that the underdeveloped countries could grow.   Now, looking back over a quarter of a century, it seems fair to say that the earlier view of the underdeveloped countries condemned to poverty and stagnation through the 'vicious circles' seems to be in need of a considerable revision.   According to the World Bank Report, during the period 1950–75, per capita income of the underdeveloped countries as a group has increased by almost 3% a year, with the annual growth rates accelerating from 2% in the 1950s to 3·4% in the 1960s.

[1] *World Development Report 1978*, World Bank 1978, Table I: Basic Indicators. Communist China is said to have a per capita income of $410 which would place her among the 'Middle Income Countries' among the underdeveloped countries. For earlier figures, see *Per Capita National Product of Fifty-five Countries: 1952–4*, United Nations Statistical Papers, Series E, no. 4, 1957; and *Trends in Developing Countries*, World Bank 1971, pt. 3.

This is an impressive achievement in the face of a rapid population growth at the rate of 2·5% a year during that period. Historically, the growth rates in per capita incomes attained by the underdeveloped countries compare very favourably with the recorded growth rates of the present-day developed countries during the period of industrialization—including a very rapidly growing country such as Japan.[1]

The inadequacy of the earlier view of the underdeveloped countries arises not only from its pessimistic assessment of their growth capacity but also from its attempt to make sweeping generalizations about them. The truth of the matter is that the underdeveloped countries are a highly diverse collection of countries which cannot be fitted into a simple theoretical scheme. The World Bank's attempt to divide them into two groups merely serves to highlight this diversity since there are considerable individual differences within each of the two groups.

Among the 'Low Income Countries', the slow growth of some countries, particularly in Africa, may arise from the fact that they are still at the earlier stages of transition from the traditional subsistence society to the exchange economy and do not as yet possess the necessary economic framework and social infra-structure to support rapid growth. Economic stagnation in other countries, whether in Africa, Asia or Latin America, is attributable to political instability and the lack of a reasonable degree of law and order, particularly in the rural districts. The slow growth of some of the South Asian countries such as Bangladesh or India may be plausibly explained in terms of population pressure aggravating poverty. But even here, one should bear in mind that population pressure on land cannot be considered without reference to agricultural techniques and government policies to encourage agricultural productivity. Where governments have pursued inappropriate policies of encouraging capital-intensive manufacturing industries at the expense of labour-intensive types of agriculture, they tend to aggravate the consequences of an unfavourable land-man ratio.

The 'Middle Income Countries' are equally diverse. They include countries such as Argentina which have long been established at a middle level of income and have nevertheless failed to achieve satisfactory growth due to political instability and inappropriate economic policies. They also include many countries which started at a much lower level of income and have risen to the middle income

[1] *World Development Report 1978*, p. 3.

level through rapid growth. Some of these countries have obtained rapid growth through the possession of oil and other mineral exports; others through the expansion of agricultural production and the diversification of primary exports; and a small but growing group of countries through the expansion of manufactured exports. Starting with labour-intensive manufacture such as textiles, this last group of countries has graduated to the exports of sophisticated manufactures and capital goods. In particular, the contrast between the slow growth of a country like Argentina and the rapid and indeed spectacular growth of countries like Taiwan and Korea emphasizes the inadequacy of the conventional approach to underdevelopment in terms of poverty, population pressure and 'vicious circles'. Thanks to her abundant land, Argentina has long enjoyed the highest per capita income level among Latin American countries, which in their turn, have a distinctly higher level of per capita incomes than the Asian and the African countries. Yet this favourable initial condition has failed to promote rapid growth in Argentina. On the other hand, Taiwan and Korea started in the 1950s with low per capita incomes typical of Asian countries and moreover have population densities on land as high or higher than India and Bangladesh. Yet Taiwan and Korea have transformed themselves into the 'success stories' of economic development through appropriate policies of raising agricultural productivity and expanding manufactured exports. Other rapidly growing countries such as Brazil, Mexico, Thailand, Malaysia and Ivory Coast also started out with low per capita incomes typical of their respective regions. If one could draw any generalizations about the fast-growing countries in spite of their diverse initial starting points, they all seem to have succeeded in expanding their agricultural production, both of food and non-food crops and their export production, both primary exports and manufactured exports.

The underlying theoretical presumption of the 'vicious circles' approach to the underdeveloped countries is that their low capacity to save is the most important constraint to their development. This view seemed plausible in the 1950s, when the underdeveloped countries were typically saving about 5% to 7% of their national income. Thus Professor Rostow specified the rise in the savings and investment ratio to no less than 10% of the national income as one of the conditions of the 'take-off' into sustained growth. Professor Lewis maintained that the conversion of a country from being a 5% saver to a 12% saver was 'the central problem in the theory of

economic growth'.[1]   However, these pronouncements were soon
overtaken by the events. According to the World Bank *Report*, even
the Low Income Countries were saving 11·6% of their GDP in 1960
and this ratio rose to 15·6% in 1975. The Middle Income Countries
saved 17·8% of their GDP in 1960 and 22·1% in 1975. Further,
there does not appear to be any close relationship between the rates
of growth in the GDP of the two groups of countries and their
average rates of domestic investment including the inflow of outside
capital resources. During the period 1960–75, the average annual
rate of growth in the GDP of the Middle Income Countries was 6%,
twice as fast as the 3·1% growth rate for the Low Income Countries.
This difference appears to be too large to be accounted for simply in
terms of differences in investment ratios: 20·2% of the GDP for the
Middle Income Countries as against 14·7% for the Low Income
Countries in 1960; and 26·1% as against 19·1% respectively in
1975.[2] The rate of growth seems to depend not merely on the supply
of savings, but on the capacity to invest the available resources
productively.

It has been pointed out earlier that the per capita income of a
country does not give an accurate measure of the representative
standard of living of the mass of its population when the total
national income is unequally distributed. Recently, there has been a
considerable growth of interest in the problems of income distribution
in the underdeveloped countries. The old pessimism concerning their
economic growth is now succeeded by the new pessimism that
economic growth by itself may not alleviate the problem of poverty
in the underdeveloped countries and that the process of rapid growth
may by-pass or even worsen the situation of the poorer section of
the people in these countries. Some have suggested that the aims of
economic development should be redefined so as to give priority to
the goal of equalizing the distribution of incomes over that of increasing the total national output and income.

---

[1] W. W. Rostow, 'The take-off into self-sustained growth', *Economic Journal*,
March 1956; W. A. Lewis, *Theory of Economic Growth*, London 1959, pp. 225–6.
[2] *World Development Report 1978*, p. 6, Text Table 8. This lack of association
between the rates of growth and the rates of investment is borne out by other
studies. For instance, Professor Reynolds, in his recent study of fifteen fast-
growing developing countries (most of which are in the World Bank's Middle
Income group) for the earlier period of 1950–65, found that the rate of gross
investment for these countries was, if anything, slightly below the average rate
for all the underdeveloped countries. cf. L. G. Reynolds, *Image and Reality in
Economic Development*, New Haven, Conn. 1977, p. 263.

Now, it may be readily accepted that in spite of the rapid economic growth during the past decades, there still remains a considerable core of poverty in the underdeveloped countries. The 'growthmanship' of the 1950s and 1960s erred in putting too much emphasis on only one side of the complex problem of economic development. But this does not mean that we should make the opposite mistake of concentrating only on the problem of income distribution to the neglect of the problem of increasing productive efficiency and total output.

To begin with, it should be pointed out that the quality of statistics concerning income distribution in the underdeveloped countries is still rather poor. The primary sources of data are sample surveys in different countries, conducted for different purposes. The information is fragmentary and does not easily lend itself to international comparisons on a uniform basis. Further, in the context of the underdeveloped countries, we are interested not only in cross-section comparisons at a given point of time but also in the changes in income distribution over a period of time during which economic growth is taking place. Time series data on the income distribution in the underdeveloped countries are rudimentary.

Next, it is necessary to draw a distinction between two concepts of income distribution, reflecting two different approaches to 'the problem of poverty' in the underdeveloped countries. If we are primarily concerned with alleviating poverty in a material sense in order to reduce hunger and disease, we would be interested in income distribution in an absolute sense. In the context of an individual country, this is defined in terms of the absolute amount of income accruing to a given section of its population, say, the poorest 40%. At an international level, this approach focuses attention on the problem of raising the 'floor' in the material level of living available to the mass of the people in the underdeveloped countries. If, on the other hand, we are primarily concerned with the problem of easing internal or international tensions with the associated feeling of discontent and 'the revolution of rising expectations', then we would be interested in income distribution in a relative sense. For an individual country, this is defined in terms of the percentage share of the total income accruing to a given section of the population compared with other groups. At the international level, this approach focuses attention on 'the widening gap' between the per capita incomes of the developed and the underdeveloped countries, as distinct from the absolute level of material standards of living available to the latter.

The World Bank economists have approached the concept of income distribution in an absolute sense by drawing a 'poverty line' at a per income level, considered to be necessary to meet the basic needs of life and estimating the number of people in the underdeveloped countries living below the poverty line.[1] In an earlier study for the year 1969, they estimated that 370 million people would be living in absolute poverty if the poverty line was drawn at the per capita income of $50, and the number would be raised to 578 million if the line was drawn at $75. In their more recent study, they seem to have adopted a different basis for defining the poverty line: it is now drawn at the corrected international purchasing power of $200 in 1970 prices (equivalent to $279 in 1975 prices). On this basis, it is estimated there were some 770 million people in the underdeveloped countries living in absolute poverty in 1975. Using alternative assumptions about future rates of growth in population and income, the number of people living in absolute poverty is projected to decline to 600 million or to 260 million in the year 2000.

Whatever our views about the future trends, the past pattern of economic growth in the underdeveloped countries provides a useful perspective to the current estimates of their poverty. It will be remembered that during the 1950s, per capita incomes of $50 to $100 were thought to be the typical level of income for the *whole* of the population in the underdeveloped countries. Allowing for the changes in the purchasing power of money, that income level seems to be roughly comparable with the minimum income now adopted for the purpose of drawing the poverty line. This would suggest that although a large core of poverty still remains, considerable numbers of the population in the underdeveloped countries have benefited from economic growth during the past twenty-five years and that there has been some improvement in the representative 'floor' of living for the mass of the people. For instance, there has been a decline in infant mortality and a rise in life expectancy among the Low Income Countries during the period 1960–75.[2] It should also be pointed out that a very large proportion of the 770 million currently estimated living in absolute poverty are concentrated in a few South Asian countries such as India, Bangladesh and Indonesia

[1] cf. H. Chenery *et al.*, *Redistribution with Growth*, Oxford University Press 1974, Table 1.2, p. 12, and *World Development Report 1978*, Text Table 34, p. 33. For the definition of the current poverty line, see *Prospects for Developing Countries 1978-85*, World Bank, November 1977, pp. 7–8.
[2] *World Development Report 1978*, Text Table 10, p. 7.

which, because of their large population bases, help to swell the number of people living in absolute poverty. This, however, suggests that the task of alleviating poverty is still largely a matter of raising productive efficiency and increasing total output rather than merely redistributing the existing output or assets. The population of these countries would merely receive their present low per capita incomes if their total national incomes were equally redistributed.

Let us now turn to the question of income distribution in a relative sense within the individual underdeveloped countries. In the absence of detailed statistics on the subject, one has to be content with the estimates of the share of income accruing to a fairly large section of the people, such as the poorest 40% of the population. Thus the World Bank study divides the underdeveloped countries into three groups: countries with high, moderate or low inequality of income distribution according as the lowest 40% of their population receive less than 12% of the total income, between 12% and 17% of the total income, or 17% or more of the total income. Two points may be made. First, in the context of economic growth, high relative inequality in income distribution does not mean that the income of the lowest 40% is reduced in an absolute sense. Thus Mexico and Brazil, for example, experienced an increase in inequality in terms of relative shares while the income of the lowest 40% grew by about 6% per annum in both cases. Secondly, there is no evidence to support the view that higher rates of growth inevitably generate greater inequality. Thus, Taiwan and Korea, the two countries which have achieved the fastest rate of growth, are also among the countries with a low degree of income inequality.[1] Greater income inequality may have occurred in particular underdeveloped countries with or without rapid growth and even under the slogans for promoting economic equality. But in the present circumstances of the underdeveloped countries, there seems to be no general reason why a greater rate of growth should increase income inequality. Much will depend on the policies pursued; so long as governments of the underdeveloped countries pursue import substitution policies favouring inappropriate domestic manufacturing industries which tend to retard growth and at the same time discriminate against the poorer section of the people in agriculture, there would still seem to be a considerable scope for promoting both growth and equality in income distribution by reversing these policies.

[1] Chenery et al., *Redistribution with Growth*. See particularly chapter 1 by M. S. Ahluwalia, Tables I.1 and I.2, pp. 10–16.

At the international level, the question of relative income distribution is posed in terms of 'the widening gap' in per capita incomes between the developed and the underdeveloped countries. It is now argued that international aid to the underdeveloped countries should not slacken simply because of the rise in the absolute level of per capita income; that more aid is necessary to reduce the widening relative gap in income levels. In the perspective of the 1950s, when the underdeveloped countries were thought to have a per capita income of about $100 compared to $1000 for the developed countries, it looked as though this widening gap was inevitable. By simple arithmetic, the poorer countries would have to grow ten times as fast as the richer countries merely to maintain the initial gap in income of $900. Yet as we have seen from the recent World Bank figures, some of the underdeveloped countries, now reclassified as Middle Income Countries, such as Singapore and Venezuela, are already having per capita incomes comparable to the poorer Industrialized Countries. It does not seem at all improbable that in the near future some of the rapidly growing developing countries such as Taiwan, South Korea, Brazil and Mexico will be overtaking the laggard Industrial Countries such as Italy or the UK. This merely brings home the misleading nature of the overall statistical averages applied to two heterogenous groups of countries broadly classified as 'developed' and 'underdeveloped'. Indeed, the 'widening gap' in income exists to the same extent among the underdeveloped countries themselves as between the ninety-two developing countries as a group and the Industrialized Countries.

The widespread concern with the problem of the widening relative gap in incomes shows that 'the problem of poverty' of the underdeveloped country is not a single problem, but a complex of problems. On one side, there is what may be called the objective problem of poverty and inability to obtain the basic material needs of life which may be measured in terms of the absolute level of per capita income. On the other side, there is the subjective problem of discontent of the underdeveloped countries with their existing international status. This arises not only from an inability to fulfil economic desires such as the desire to imitate the higher standards of private consumption and public social welfare set by the advanced countries, but also from the deeper psychological and political drives to raise their national prestige and obtain equal status and international esteem with the advanced countries. This transcends any statistical measurement even in terms of the relative gap in income levels.

I began by saying that there are two main forces behind the study of the underdeveloped countries: the desire to understand the nature and causes of their poverty and the desire to show the need to do something urgently about it. Post-war writing on the subject has been dominated by the second motive. This is true not only of the voluminous and expanding literature produced by the various agencies of the United Nations and various governmental bodies, but also of the writings of some of the academic economists themselves. Faced with the pressing human and political problems of the underdeveloped countries, they also became impatient with dispassionate academic inquiry and have frequently taken on the role of the champions and spokesmen for the underdeveloped countries. While this is understandable enough, the practical usefulness of development policies will depend on the soundness and realism of the theoretical analyses on which they are based. Here, as we have seen, the broad experiences of economic development in the underdeveloped countries during the past twenty-five years have cast considerable doubts on the earlier simplistic view that economic development is basically a matter of increasing the supply of savings and capital funds available for investment and that the development economist should mainly concern himself with urging the developed countries to transfer more capital resources to the underdeveloped countries either through international aid or through concessions in international trade. It now appears that economic development is not simply a matter of increasing the supply of savings and investible resources but crucially depends on the capacity to use these resources productively. Our knowledge of the causes of the increase in the productivity of resources in the underdeveloped countries is still imperfect; and whatever our views about what ought to be the proper goals of development policy, a better understanding of how the underdeveloped economic systems work and how the productivity of their resources may be affected by the mode of their working would still seem to be essential.

The aim of this book is to give an introduction to the economics of the underdeveloped or the developing countries using the traditional academic approach of dispassionate analysis and clarification. Within the limited scope of a small book, I have tried my best to give a broad picture of the different types of countries at different stages of development. The earlier Chapters 3 to 5 trace the growth of the exchange economy, the wage economy and the domestic market for capital funds in the setting of the underdeveloped countries which still have natural resources for economic expansion. This helps to bring out the changes in the internal economic organization of the developing countries without being obscured by the problem of population pressure. In Chapters 6 and 7, the various theories of capital requirements to overcome the vicious circle of poverty are examined in the setting of countries subject to population pressure. Chapters 8 and 9 are concerned with Agriculture and International Trade, which seems to be the two main factors in explaining why some underdeveloped countries grew faster than others in the post-war decades. Since this book was first written some fifteen years ago, the spectrum of the general levels of economic development to be found among the underdeveloped countries has widened and in general I have kept the main focus of the book on the earlier stages of development and on the Low Income Countries rather than on the later stages of development and on the Middle Income or the Semi-Industrialized Countries.

2

THE EXPANSION OF EXPORTS AND

THE GROWTH OF POPULATION

The opening up of the underdeveloped countries
A popular idea of the underdeveloped country is of a closed society
stagnating in traditional isolation, like Tibet before the Chinese
annexation. Paradoxically enough, such a society in complete isolation would have few of the typical problems of the present-day
underdeveloped countries. It would have a low and stagnant income
per capita, but this would not matter if its inhabitants were blissfully
unaware of the higher standards of living in the outside world. With
no foreign trade, it would not have the problem of dependence on a
few primary export commodities whose prices fluctuate violently in
the world market. With no foreign enterprises operating within it,
and no colonial rule, it would be free from real or imaginary griev-
ances against 'foreign economic domination' and 'colonial exploitation'. And with a high death rate to match a high birth rate, it would
not have to contend with the problem of population pressure as the
population would be fairly stable or fluctuating around a constant
size.
\ In contrast, the typical problems of the present-day underdeveloped
countries arise, not because these countries are in the traditional state
of isolation, but because they have been 'opened up' to outside forces,
in the form of foreign trade, investment and colonial rule.\ The
expansion of export production and the spread of the money economy
have disrupted in varying degrees the economic self-sufficiency of the
traditional 'subsistence economy'. The introduction of an orderly
framework of administration by the colonial governments and the
provision of basic public services, especially public health, have
reduced the death rates and caused a rapid growth of population.
This has disrupted the traditional balance between population,

natural resources and technology. Of course, the traditional society still persists in varying degrees in most underdeveloped countries in the form of the 'subsistence sector', and, as we shall see, this dominates the economic life of many countries, particularly in Africa. But it is still true to say that the typical present-day problems of these countries arise, not from traditional isolation but from modern changes. In a sense all underdeveloped countries are at different stages in the long transition period (or the 'pre-take-off' period) in which they are having to adapt to a continuing process of rapid and disruptive changes. Their problems arise from their difficulties in making satisfactory adjustments to these changes.

In this chapter I shall make a preliminary survey of the two major forces of change which have had and still continue to have a profound impact on the economic and social life of the underdeveloped countries. The first is the expansion of primary exports and the growth of the money economy. The second is the growth of population.

Expansion of exports

I shall begin by clearing up two points about the expansion of primary exports from the underdeveloped countries.

First, it is frequently described as the 'nineteenth-century' pattern of international trade. Those who use this epithet may merely mean that it is associated with the nineteenth-century belief in free trade, but the general impression created is that the expansion of primary exports from the underdeveloped countries was historically important only in the nineteenth century. This is rather misleading. It is true that this process started in the latter half of the nineteenth century and owed much to the nineteenth-century revolution in transport such as the railways, the steamship and, in the case of the Asian countries whose exports expanded fastest during this period, to the opening of the Suez Canal. But what is not generally realized is that the greatest expansion of primary exports from the under-developed countries of Africa and Latin America has taken place in the first half of the twentieth century. Contrary to the general impression that primary export expansion slackened off in the inter-war period, P. Lamartine Yates has calculated that the African and Latin American countries have expanded the total value of their exports ten-fold during the period 1913–53.[1]

Secondly, the primary exporting countries and the underdeveloped

[1] P. Lamartine Yates, *Forty Years of Foreign Trade*, London 1959, Table 102, pp. 160–2.

countries are frequently identified with each other, and the relative prices between primary exports as a whole and manufactured exports as a whole have been used to measure the gains from international trade to the underdeveloped countries. This again is not accurate. While all underdeveloped countries may be primary exporters, not all primary exporters are underdeveloped countries. The high-income countries of Australasia and North America are also important primary exporters. Currently, the developed countries produce some two-fifths of the world's exports of primary commodities excluding oil. On the other hand, agricultural products (excluding oil and minerals) contributed to only 43% of the total exports of the underdeveloped countries in 1960 and this share fell to 27% in 1975.[1]

In spite of this, however, individually many of these countries may depend on the export of a few primary products. This has aroused considerable fears about the vulnerability of these 'export economies' to short-run fluctuations in the world market demand for primary products. It has been argued that this not only introduces a serious instability into the consumption and living standards of these countries but also creates formidable difficulties for maintaining a steady flow of investment for long-term economic development. This has led to various proposals for commodity stabilization schemes culminating in the recent proposal for an 'Integrated Programme for Commodities' put forward by the United Nations Conference on Trade and Development (UNCTAD) in 1974. However, it should be pointed out that there is a considerable body of empirical research suggesting that the *prima facie* case for suspecting that the underdeveloped countries suffer from the short-run export instability to a greater extent than the advanced countries is not borne out by factual evidence.[2] Beyond this problem of short-run economic stability, the impact of the outside economic forces on the underdeveloped countries has given rise to two longer-run problems.

The first problem is the relation between the expansion of primary exports and the long-term economic development of the underdeveloped countries. Some of the orthodox economists were inclined to assume too readily that the expansion of international trade would

[1] See *World Development Report 1978*, Text Table 25, and the Background Paper no. 5 for that report entitled *The Changing Composition of Developing Countries' Exports*, World Bank, September 1978.
[2] See J. D. Coppock, *International Economic Instability*, New York 1962; A. I. Macbean, *Export Instability and Economic Development*, London 1966; and O. Knudsen and A. Parnes, *Trade Instability and Economic Development*, Lexington, Mass., 1975. This question will be discussed in Chapters 9 and 10 below.

automatically transmit economic growth to the underdeveloped countries, and the 'specialization' in the production of those primary products most suited to their resources would automatically raise their general level of skills and productivity and lead to a more productive combination of resources. This would pave the way for further economic development. Nowadays, the pendulum has swung to the opposite extreme, not only among the political leaders of the developing countries but among professional economists also. It is now generally assumed that the expansion of primary exports is highly unlikely ever to provide a satisfactory basis of continuous economic growth for the underdeveloped countries. I shall examine not only the older generalization but also the newer generalization which is a reaction against the older view.

The second problem arises from the fact that the expansion of primary exports in the underdeveloped countries generally took place through the agency of foreign-owned enterprises operating within these countries and, until recently, under colonial rule for most of the Asian and African countries. The problem of the relationship between the expansion of primary exports and long-term economic development is therefore considerably complicated by the problems of subjective discontent concerning 'foreign economic domination' and 'colonial exploitation'. To study these problems I shall have to go beyond the overall values of the exports of the underdeveloped countries as geographical units, and analyse how the proceeds from these geographical exports were distributed between foreign and domestic participants in export production. In the case of peasant export commodities, the participants were the foreign export–import firms and the domestic peasant producers. In the case of mining and plantation exports, the foreign participation covered not only capital investment and skilled labour but also in many cases unskilled labour from other underdeveloped countries; the domestic participation was mainly confined to such indigenous unskilled labour as might be employed in the mines and plantations. These different patterns and the differing extent of domestic participation in export production are important, not only from the point of view of income distribution but also from the point of view of long-term economic development. First, the distribution of incomes between the foreign and domestic participants would have some effect on the proportion of incomes reinvested locally and spent on domestically produced goods, compared with the 'leakages' abroad in the form of imports and remittances of the earnings of the foreign participants. Secondly, if we wish to find out how far the expansion of primary export production has affected the skills and productivity of the indigenous people of the underdeveloped countries, we shall have to to go beyond the pattern of distribution of incomes to the distribution of productive activities and economic roles. We can then look for the particular features in the past pattern of primary export expansion that have been unfavourable for the maintenance of long-term economic growth, and consider whether these characteristic features are the inevitable concomitant of future expansion in primary export production for some of the underdeveloped countries.

With these questions in view, I shall devote the next three chapters to the study of the expansion of exports first from the peasant sector and then from the mining and plantation sector. I shall outline the typical patterns of the growth of the market economy, not only in the markets for commodities but also in the markets for labour and capital funds. I shall start from the early phase of export expansion and bring the story up to the present time when the reaction against the past economic pattern has led to various nationalistic policies of economic development being adopted by the governments of the newly independent developing countries. The more recent issues of international trade and economic development will be discussed in Chapter 9.

The growth of population

Let us now turn to the other major change which has affected the underdeveloped countries—the growth of population. An underdeveloped country in its traditional state of isolation tends to have a fairly stable population with a high birth rate and a high death rate balancing out over the long run. Although accurate information is not available, the most probable estimate seems to be that, before their contact with the West, many underdeveloped countries in Asia and Africa had high birth rates in the region of 4% per annum matched by equally high death rates of about 4%. Starting from the initial position of high birth and death rates, I shall describe the typical pattern of population growth with three stages or sets of factors that reduce the death rate while the birth rate continues at its high initial level.[1]

First, the introduction of a modern administration improving law and order and eliminating local warfare, and the introduction of modern transport and communication eliminating local famines and

[1] cf. W. A. Lewis, *The Theory of Economic Growth*, London 1959, ch. 6.

spreading trading in foodstuffs, can by themselves reduce the death rate of an underdeveloped country by as much as 1% per annum. So if the birth rate remains unchanged, population will be increasing at 1% per annum. Secondly, the introduction of public health measures controlling epidemic and endemic diseases such as plague, smallpox, cholera, malaria, yellow fever (and eventually tuberculosis) can reduce the death rate by at least another 1%. So if the birth rate remains the same, the population of the underdeveloped country will be increasing at some 2% per annum at the end of this second stage. Thirdly, the spread of individual medical attention and the increase in the number of doctors and hospitals can bring down the death rate by another 1%, depending on the age structure of the population. In this final stage, therefore, if the birth rate remains the same at 4% and the death rate is reduced to 1% per annum, the maximum possible rate of growth in population will approach 3% per annum.

Most of the underdeveloped countries have passed through the first two stages and are well into the final phase with the rate of population increase between 2% and 3% per annum. Some have attained or even exceeded the 3% rate of population growth suggesting that the general assumption of 4% maximum birth rate is too low for them. During the period 1950–60, the average rate of population growth for the underdeveloped countries as a group was 2·2% per annum. The fastest rate of population growth was recorded for Latin America with the average annual rate of 2·8% while Africa and the Far East showed rates of growth of 2·2% and 2·1% respectively.[1] India, which until the last census in 1961 had a population growth of 1·4% per annum, now seems to have passed the 2% mark, mainly due to better control of malaria. So when people speak of the 'population explosion' in the underdeveloped countries, they mean that the populations of these countries are not only increasing but increasing at a faster rate of growth year by year with a high rate of acceleration. An extreme example of this is the case of Ceylon where DDT has wiped out malaria, reducing the death rate from 2·2% to 1·2% in seven years from 1945 to 1952—a fall which took seventy years in England and Wales.[2]

Although the rate of population growth is clearly very important, two other factors must be taken into account in studying the problem of population pressure in the underdeveloped countries.

[1] United Nations, *World Economic Survey 1963*, pt. 1, p. 20, Table 2–2.
[2] PEP, *World Population and Resources*, London 1955, p. 12.

The first is the population density in relation to natural resources and technology. Population density in a significant sense cannot be measured simply by taking the number of people per square mile. It will depend on a number of factors such as the quality of agricultural land, climate and water supply, the existence of mineral resources, the possibilities of hydroelectric power, to name a few; and also, very importantly, on the level of productivity and technology. Europe and Asia, for example (excluding USSR from both), are estimated to have the same amount of agricultural area per person of 1·5 acres, but with widely differing standards of living or 'population densities' in the economic sense. But taking the level of technology to mean the indigenous methods of agricultural production and making allowances for obvious differences in natural resources, it is still possible to say that there are very significant differences in population densities between the different parts of the underdeveloped world. Compared, for example, with the agricultural area per person of 1·5 acres in Asia, Latin America is estimated to have 6·9 acres, and Africa 10·6 acres of agricultural area per person.[1] In a relatively sparsely populated region like Latin America, even a high population growth rate will not for the time being give rise to the problem of population pressure. In fact, many would regard it as a favourable factor for future economic development. In contrast, with the dense population of China even a small population growth rate will create formidable problems of population pressure.

There are two main types of underdeveloped country with high population densities. Firstly, there are the long settled agricultural countries such as India, China or Egypt. In a sense, their present population problem is due to their successful development as agricultural countries in the past. This enabled them to support a dense population before it started growing in the modern period. Secondly, there are the island plantation economies, such as the West Indies, Fiji, Mauritius or Ceylon. Here, immigrant labour has been brought from outside to work in the mines and plantations to add to the indigenous population. Population pressure subsequently developed, helped by the relative ease with which diseases such as malaria can be wiped out from the islands. In general, the first group of countries tend to have a larger population base than the second—contrast India's 569 millions in 1971 with Fiji's 0·5 million.

This brings us to the second important factor to be taken into

[1] PEP, *World Population and Resources*, London 1955, p. 50, and chs. 2 and 3.

account in studying the population problems of the underdeveloped countries, that is the absolute size of the population base. When giving aid, countries like India with a huge population base clearly present a more formidable problem than countries with a smaller population, even if the smaller populations are increasing at a faster rate. Even before 1951, when the rate of increase was relatively slow, India's population was increasing at the rate of 5 millions a year: currently, at the estimated growth rate of 2·4% per annum, it is increasing at 12 millions a year. The size of the population base, however, is also of great importance as it affects the total scale of the economy; this is relevant for the success of industrialization programmes. Of course, the size of the domestic market of a country does not depend only on the numbers, but also on the income level of its inhabitants. But given the same low level of per capita incomes, a country like India offers a more favourable environment for setting up heavy capital goods industries which depend so much on the economies of scale for their success. In contrast, a thickly populated country with a small population base such as Ceylon seems to be especially handicapped by the smallness of its market.[1] Finally, considering the absolute size of the population base serves to remind us that while the large populations of the advanced countries have grown up after, and as a consequence of, economic development, the large populations of the underdeveloped countries exist before development: this makes development not only more desirable but also more difficult.[2]

In broad terms, the population problem of the densely populated underdeveloped countries is a vivid illustration of the Malthusian theory. On a closer analysis, I would add three qualifications.

(1) The Malthusian proposition that the growth of population will exceed the growth of food supplies underrates technological innovations in food production, including the opening up of new territories and international trade. That was why the advanced Western countries were able to escape from its direful predictions. In a sense, the theories of economic development for the overpopulated underdeveloped countries are built on this qualification. They are based on the idea that while there is a maximum limit to population growth, say 3% per annum, the possible rate of increase in output owing to

[1] J. R. Hicks, *Essays in World Economics*, London 1959, pp. 207–8.
[2] S. Kuznets, *Underdeveloped Countries and the Pre-industrial Phase in the Advanced Countries*, World Population Conference, 1954, Papers, vol. V.

technical innovation and capital accumulation can exceed this maximum rate of population growth, keeping the Malthusian devil at bay until the birth rates in the underdeveloped countries begin to fall, as they have fallen in the European countries and are falling in countries like Japan.

(2) The Malthusian theory is based on too rigid a causal connection between the rate of growth in food supply and population growth. According to the theory, population will not grow unless the food supply or the standard of living rises above the minimum subsistence level. But as we have seen, the population in many underdeveloped countries has grown very rapidly without any appreciable rise in per capita income, mainly owing to medical improvements reducing death rates. If the Malthusian theory has underrated the possibilities of technical improvements in food production, it has also underrated the medical improvements reducing death rates. The possibility that even a population struggling at a minimum subsistence level could grow in the short run simply by medical improvements entirely unconnected with the general standard of life adds to the seriousness of the problem in the modern setting. There is a gleam of hope, however, if we are willing to believe that the technical improvements in medicine which are at present reducing death rates only can be eventually extended to reduce birth rates by the invention of simpler and cheaper methods of birth-control.

(3) The Malthusian theory is formulated in the setting of a more or less developed wage economy. According to it, with given natural resources and technology, the saturation point in a country's population will be reached when the level of wages, determined by the marginal product of labour, is equal to the minimum subsistence level. But in many underdeveloped countries, the problem of population pressure takes place in the setting of the subsistence economy before the development of the money and the wage economy. In this setting, with an extended family system, many people whose marginal product on the land is below the subsistence level can continue to exist at that level because the total output from land is shared among the members of the extended family. That is to say, with the same natural resources and technology, the saturation point of population in a subsistence economy is larger than that of a wage economy (without public poor relief) because it is determined by the equality of the average product of labour to the minimum subsistence level. Many people who would have been unemployed and starved in a wage economy are maintained in 'disguised' unemployment by their

relatives as part of a traditional social security system. As we shall see, much has been made of this phenomenon of 'disguised unemployment' in the post-war theories of economic development as a concealed source of saving. But there is one point which is not always appreciated. In so far as we believe that economic development can take place only through the introduction of a modern money and wage economy which entails the dismantling of the traditional social security system of the subsistence economy, the overpopulated underdeveloped countries in a process of transition have to meet a double problem of population increase. In addition to their natural rate of increase in population they also have to find jobs for those who are displaced from the subsistence economy when the development of the exchange economy and economic individualism reduces the size of the 'family' as a social security unit.

To sum up, the problem of population pressure in the underdeveloped countries has three aspects: (1) the rate of growth of the population; (2) the existing density of population; and (3) the overall magnitude of the population base. In these terms, the population situation in the underdeveloped countries shows considerable variation. At one end of the scale there are the underdeveloped countries which are relatively thinly populated and are not yet suffering from population pressure. These include some of the South-East Asian countries such as Burma, Thailand, Malaysia and the Outer Islands of Indonesia; many of the African countries with the notable exception of Egypt; and most of the Latin American countries. The magnitude of the population base in these countries is also small and is below 50 millions, with the exception of Brazil, which is, however, still thinly populated. At the other end of the scale there are the densely populated countries suffering from varying degrees of population pressure. These include islands with plantation economies such as the West Indies, Mauritius and Ceylon where the population pressure is acute although the magnitude of the population base is fairly small; and the thickly populated countries of Asia and the Middle East with much larger population bases. The population pressure problem is most formidable in countries like India and Pakistan which are not only densely populated, but have a large population base and are now entering into a phase of rapid population growth above the 2% annual rate.

Post-war theories about the developing countries tend to be dominated by the model of the overpopulated countries. But large areas of the underdeveloped world such as Latin America, South-East Asia and various parts of Africa started with sparse populations in relation to their natural resources and are not yet suffering from population pressure. We need, therefore, at least two main theoretical models, one for the countries with no significant population pressure, and another for the overpopulated countries. For certain purposes involving the analysis of the economies of scale, we shall find it useful to sub-divide the overpopulated countries into two groups: those like India with a large population base, say over 50 millions; and those like Ceylon and Mauritius with a small population base.

In the next two chapters, I shall be mainly working on the basis of the model of the underdeveloped countries without significant population pressure. I have done this not only to give a more balanced picture of the subject, which is normally dominated by the model of the overpopulated countries, but also because the important structural problems arising out of the growth of the money economy and the wage economy through the expansion of primary export production can be most clearly seen when isolated from the problem of population pressure. I shall return to the model of overpopulated countries when we examine the post-war theories of economic development in Chapters 6, 7 and 8.

3

PEASANT EXPORTS AND THE
GROWTH OF THE MONEY ECONOMY

The importance of the peasant sector

Although peasant exports such as rice, cocoa, palm oil or cotton have a modest share in the total value of primary exports from the underdeveloped world as a whole,[1] it is important to study the expansion of peasant export production for at least three reasons.

First, peasant families, combining the roles of consumers and producers, are the basic units of the subsistence economy and are therefore of central importance in studying the impact of outside economic forces on the people of the underdeveloped countries. In addition, the expansion of peasant exports is one of the best documented parts of the process of economic change in the underdeveloped countries, and we can build up a fairly clear picture of the response of the indigenous people to economic incentives. This gives us a good basis to judge various generalizations about the economic behaviour of the people of the underdeveloped countries in other contexts.

Secondly, from the viewpoint of the indigenous people in the

---

[1] Important peasant exports are confined to a few countries of Asia and Africa, such as Burma, Thailand, Ghana, Nigeria, Uganda, etc. Latin America has little or no peasant exports. The importance of the mines and plantations in the total primary exports of the underdeveloped countries as a group can be seen from the fact that in 1953, the mineral products alone contributed to over a third of the total primary exports of the group. Among agricultural products, plantation output dominates in the exports of coffee, sugar, tea, sisal, etc. Rubber is a predominantly plantation export although smallholders in Malaya contribute an important part of the output. Cocoa and palm oil, which are peasant products in West Africa, are plantation products in Brazil, Indonesia and Malaya. cf. P. Lamartine Yates, *Forty Years of Foreign Trade*, London 1959, Table 32A, p. 240.

subsistence economy, peasant production is the main alternative to wage employment, not only in the mines and plantations, but also in manufacturing industry. Thus the major process of economic development by which labour from the subsistence economy is drawn into wage employment cannot be studied without taking into account the alternative opportunities (or lack of them) as self-employed peasant producers.

Thirdly, the expansion of peasant export production is so important and spectacular in a number of Asian and African underdeveloped countries that it is worth studying for its own sake. For instance, using 1870 as the base, the value of peasant rice exports from Burma and Thailand increased some 10 to 13 times by 1913, and up to about 20 times in the late 1920s before the onset of the Great Depression. Similarly, the value of Ghana's cocoa exports increased about 13 times during the 1913–53 period. During the same period Nigeria expanded her exports of oil and oil seeds by 7 times in addition to a very rapid expansion of cocoa exports. In all these countries, the physical output of the export crops followed a characteristic growth curve, rising steeply in the early phase and tapering off gradually.[1]

This rapid expansion of the peasant export sector is all the more interesting because, unlike that of the mining and plantation sector, it seems to owe little or nothing to outside economic resources. (1) Most of the foreign investment in the underdeveloped countries flowed into the mining and plantation sector where the major part of the capital requirement took the form of expensive durable equipment and fixed capital. In contrast, apart from land, peasant production required very little durable capital equipment. Its major capital requirement took the form of circulating capital or the 'subsistence fund' of food and consumers' goods required to maintain the peasants until the harvest was ready. As we shall see, in its early phase of expansion,

---

[1] cf. J. S. Furnivall, *Colonial Policy and Practice*, Cambridge 1948, Appendix I; J. C. Ingram, *Economic Change in Thailand since 1850*, Stanford 1955, ch. 3 and Appendix C; Lamartime Yates, op. cit., pp. 242–3; and the West African Institute of Economic Research, *Annual Conference*, Economic Section, Achimota 1953, pp. 96–7. Peasant exports contributed two-thirds of Burma's total exports up to 1937 and dominate her post-war exports with the decline of output from the foreign-owned mines and plantations. Cocoa contributed 50% to the value of Ghana's total exports in 1913 and 70% in 1953. Oil and oil seeds contributed 78% to the total value of Nigeria's exports in 1913. In 1953 oil and oil seeds and cocoa contributed 70% to her total exports.

peasant export production appears to have been largely 'self-financing'. Further problems of capital and financing of the peasant sector will be taken up in Chapter 5. (2) While the mining and plantation sector represents the extension of modern economic organization and technology, the peasant export sector seems to be simply an extension of the traditional economic organization and technology of the subsistence economy. Rice exports from South-East Asia, for example, represent the traditional subsistence crop whose cultivation has been expanded by traditional methods for the export market. Even in West Africa where cocoa was a new crop (introduced by peasant enterprise) the secret of its success was that it did not require a radical departure from the methods of subsistence agriculture and could therefore be readily grafted on to the traditional economy.[1] (3) While the mining and plantation sector usually recruited a large part of their unskilled labour from outside the countries in which they were located, peasant export expansion required little or no labour from abroad. In fact, the bulk of the labour was supplied from the family circle of the peasant producers. The size of the peasant holdings was usually not large enough to require hired labour from outside except in very busy seasons such as the harvest. Further, the 'family' in peasant societies embraced an extensive network of more distant relatives. For these reasons hired wage labour from outside the family circle did not become important in the peasant export sector until a later stage,[2] although there was some development of wage labour in the ancillary industries which went with peasant export expansion, such as transport and processing—for instance rice milling in South-East Asia.

The mechanics of peasant expansion

How then did this very rapid process of expansion take place? Two things were necessary to start the process. The first was the improvement in transport and communications opening up the remoter districts (and incidentally improving the law and order in these parts); the second was the establishment of foreign export–import firms to act as the middlemen between the peasants and the world market.

*European, Asian and Levantine

[1] A. McPhee, *The Economic Revolution in West Africa*, London 1926, pp. 39–40.
[2] In Ghana, the most highly developed peasant export economy in Africa, the ratio of family labour to hired labour in cocoa production was estimated to be about 5:1 in 1950 (UN Report on the *Enlargement of the Exchange Economy in Tropical Africa*, New York 1954, p. 31). Hired labour, paid in kind at harvest, was used in Burmese rice production.

The improvement in transport and communications was overwhelmingly important in many countries. The export–import firms performed two functions: to collect, process and transport the peasant produce to the foreign buyers, and to offer the peasants the inducement to increase export production by selling them imported goods. This inducement to the peasants was as important, perhaps even more important, than the other function of the firms. For in this early phase of international trade, imports were not merely a cheaper way of satisfying the *existing* wants of the peasants. Many of them were novelties hitherto unknown in the subsistence economy. By stimulating new wants among the peasants, the expansion of imports was a major dynamic force facilitating the expansion of exports. The speed with which the peasants of South-East Asia and West Africa (with their different cultural backgrounds) acquired the taste for the new imported commodities and expanded their export production in order to be able to buy them offers us concrete evidence of their capacity to respond positively to economic incentives. It casts serious doubt on popular generalizations about the limited wants and the inability of the people to respond to economic incentives. We shall meet these generalizations when we consider the factors determining the wage level in the mining and plantation sector.

With these two initial factors—the improvement in transport and communications, and the existence of the foreign export–import firms to get the peasants in touch with the world market—peasant export production expanded rapidly by extending cultivation in widening circles into the hinterland of the country. On the supply side, there were two other factors which enabled peasant export expansion to grow so quickly and on so large a scale. The first was of course the existence of unused hinterland, the jungles which could be cleared to grow the export crop. It was no accident that all the Asian and African countries which were to develop into important peasant export economies started before the expansion of trade with relatively sparse population and abundant supply of 'semi-empty' hinterland. The second concerned the source of the labour supply, which requires more careful analysis.

I have said that peasant export production did not rely on large-scale immigrant labour from abroad, and that it did not introduce any drastic changes in methods of agriculture, such as labour-saving techniques. Yet the physical output of peasant exports grew most rapidly, well above any possible natural rate of increase in working population, in the early phase of expansion when most of the labour requirement must have been supplied from within the peasant families. This suggests that initially there must have been a considerable amount of underemployed or surplus labour in these families. At first sight, this may appear surprising since the idea of rural underemployment or 'disguised unemployment' is nowadays only associated with overpopulated countries where there is insufficient work for every member of the family on the overcrowded land. But the cause of the rural underemployment which must have existed in the thinly populated peasant societies before they were opened up to trade was quite different. There was abundant waste land waiting to be cultivated, but labour remained underemployed because there was a lack of effective demand for its potential increase in output. In the initial situation, with the available surplus land and surplus labour, and with the traditional methods of cultivation, a peasant family could have produced a much larger agricultural output than it was actually producing for its own subsistence consumption. But it chose not to do so, for the simple reason that every other peasant family could do the same and there would be no one in the locality who would want to buy the surplus output. With the poor transport and communications and the rudimentary exchange system which existed before the opening up of the export trade, the local and domestic market of the underdeveloped countries was too narrow and unorganized to absorb their potential surplus agricultural output. At this stage, therefore, the main function of international trade was to create effective demand: it linked up the world market demand for the type of things which the peasants could produce with the surplus productive capacity the peasants had locked up in the subsistence economy.

Two concepts of the subsistence sector and the two stages of the money economy

At this stage it is necessary to distinguish the two possible meanings of the term 'subsistence' economy or sector. It can mean that the economic units within it such as the family, the village or the tribe, are self-sufficient, producing only what they require for their own consumption, and having little or no systematic exchange relationship among each other. This is the sense in which we have been using the term so far, and in our context 'subsistence' simply means non-monetary. The term also carries the suggestion that the people within the subsistence sector are living at a 'minimum subsistence level': that is to say, the resources and the technology they possess are just sufficient to keep them alive in their present numbers at the minimum level of subsistence. Clearly, the 'subsistence' sector in the first sense does not necessarily mean that the people within it are struggling at the 'minimum subsistence level' in the second sense. Indeed, the rapid expansion in exports we have been describing could not really have taken place had these particular peasant societies been really at the minimum subsistence level in the true sense before trade was opened to them. The essential lubricant which pushed the peasants so smoothly and rapidly into export production and the money economy was the existence of a considerable margin of surplus productive capacity in the form of both surplus land and surplus labour over and above their minimum subsistence requirements.

With this margin of surplus productive capacity, the peasants could take to the production of cash crops for the export market *without* reducing their subsistence output. In the South-East Asian countries, where rice was both a subsistence and an export crop, the question of reducing subsistence production did not arise. The subsistence crops of African peasant economies could either be interplanted with their export crops (such as cocoa trees) before they reached a certain age, or cultivated in rotation with export crops such as cotton and groundnuts. With the exception of Ghana in recent years, the normal pattern in many African countries still seems to be for the output of the subsistence crops and the cash crops for export to expand together.[1] In the early phase of export expansion, therefore, what the peasants were in effect doing was taking up export production as a part-time activity to obtain an extra cash income, in addition to their subsistence production of which they had already made sure. This cash income could then be spent on extra luxury items of consumption in the form of imported goods. The expansion of export production at this phase was a virtually riskless operation, requiring no other cost than extra working hours which could be provided from the initial situation of underemployment. Because, as we have seen, the 'capital requirement' in peasant production consisted mainly in the 'subsistence fund' to tide over the producers until the harvest, export expansion of this type could be mainly self-financing.

As a contrast, let us consider a different initial situation in which

[1] cf. UN Report on the *Enlargement of the Exchange Economy*, (cited above, p. 31), pp. 21–2. 'Thus in Uganda for example, where the estimates of the area under major crops are available for a number of years, the area under cotton increased between 1918 and 1950 about eleven-fold and the area under subsistence food crops about seven times.'

the peasants had to devote the whole of their time and resources to obtain a minimum subsistence level of living before the opening up of trade. Here, even if switching their resources from the subsistence to the cash crops promised some monetary gain, they would have been obliged to reduce their subsistence output to grow the export crop. This would have made their entry into export production and the money economy a hazardous undertaking with no margin to meet a possible risk of starvation if something went wrong with their cash crops. In this case, we should expect the peasants to be justifiably hesitant about leaving the security of their subsistence economy, and their export production, if any, would expand much more slowly than the actual rates of expansion we have observed in the peasant economies of South-East Asia and West Africa. This may partly account for the persistence of large subsistence sectors in the over-populated countries like India and Pakistan in spite of the fact that they have been opened up to outside economic forces much longer than the African countries. To try to explain this entirely in terms of the 'conservatism' of their peasants and social rigidities is not convincing since these factors also operate in other peasant societies where export production and the money economy have expanded at a much faster rate. The size of the margin of surplus productive capacity over the minimum subsistence requirement in the subsistence sector therefore emerges as a very important factor determining how quickly the subsistence sector can be drawn into the money economy. I have emphasized the initial population density on land as one of the determinants of this surplus productive capacity; but it also depends on other factors such as the technical efficiency of the subsistence agriculture, or the fertility and accessibility of the land under subsistence cultivation.

On this basis, I can now depict the spread of the money economy and the expansion of peasant export production in two analytically distinct phases, although they overlap a great deal in practice. In the first phase, the money economy may be considered as growing simply by bringing in an increasing number of peasant families into export production, each family producing the export crop on a spare-time basis while continuing to produce all its subsistence requirements. In the second phase, however, some peasant families will begin to 'specialize' or devote the whole of their available resources to export production, so setting up a cash demand for locally produced foodstuffs and other locally produced goods and services.

These two phases in the growth of the money economy have very different characteristics. The first phase offers certain advantages to the peasants, since the export production is a spare-time activity in addition to their subsistence production. Imports represent a net increase in consumption and a rise in the standard of living. And since their 'capital requirements' are largely provided out of the subsistence output, they are largely self-financing and need not resort to borrowing at high rates of interest from money-lenders. Similarly, their bargaining position with the middlemen is also stronger, since if the prices offered for their cash crops are not favourable, they can afford to reduce output next year (just enough to pay taxes, if any). There are two disadvantages, however, in partial commitment to the money economy. First, the peasants have not fully utilized the market opportunities open to them and could increase their income by greater 'specialization'. Secondly, the main function of money in this first phase is merely to exchange exports for imports. That is to say, the money economy is confined to foreign trade and has little or no impact on the rest of the domestic economy.

In contrast, in the second phase, the fact that some peasant families are devoting the whole of their available resources to export production obliges them to buy their food requirements from other peasant families who can now specialize in food production as a cash crop for the domestic market. That is to say, complete specialization in export production by some peasant families not only enables them to make full use of their available market opportunities, but also provides the scope for secondary rounds of economic activities which may spread widely into the rest of the economy. The money economy has now spread from the foreign trade sector to the domestic sector. Here, it may spread into the market for other locally produced consumers' goods industries in so far as they can compete with the imports. It may spread into the market for labour for these local industries and for peasant agriculture itself in so far as hired labour is required to supplement that of the family. It may spread into the market for land in so far as existing laws and customs permit free buying, selling and renting of land. These are the advantages, but the second phase in the growth of the money economy also brings to a head many of the problems latent in a situation in which peasants inexperienced in modern economic life are brought into rapid contact with the complexities of an unstable export market. In switching over from part-time to full-time production for the export market, the peasants cease to be self-financing and have to borrow from the chief source available to them—the money-lenders who charge them

high rates of interest. With their ignorance of the rapidly changing
market conditions, they tend to get heavily into debt, and where land
is alienable, they lose their land in default of loans and get reduced
to the status of tenants. And with their fixed and frequently heavy
monetary obligations in the form of debts, rents, and also government
taxes, they can no longer afford to reduce their output when the price
is lowered; they may even try to produce more to make up for the
lower price. But the inelastic nature of their supply curve aggravates
the fall in the price of their export products. With this full (if sometimes involuntary) commitment to the money economy, the peasants
now have a weaker bargaining position with the middlemen. In most
peasant export economies, the middlemen, after a long chain of intermediaries, culminate in a few large export–import firms, each buying
a large proportion of the total output of the peasants. At this stage,
therefore, there is a real danger that a few foreign-owned firms would
combine to exercise monopoly power over the peasants and shift on
to them the main impact of the fall in the world market price for the
export product.

Most of the African peasant economies, with the notable exception
of Ghana, are still largely in the first phase of the growth of the
money economy. The peasants there are only partially committed to
the production of cash crops, and the larger proportion of their
resources (about 70% of the total cultivated land and about 60% of
the total adult male labour force for the whole of tropical Africa) is
still used for subsistence production. Even in Nigeria and Uganda,
which are the most developed African peasant economies after
Ghana, over half their land and labour resources are still in the
subsistence sector.[1] Similar conditions probably exist in the Indian
peasant societies of Latin America whose exports are predominantly
from the mining and plantation sector. The main reason for the
existence of these large subsistence sectors seems to be lack of transport and communications, and the very poor marketing facilities
available to the peasant. This type of subsistence sector in Africa
which belongs to the early phase in the spread of the money economy
may be contrasted with the subsistence sectors which have persisted
in the overpopulated countries of Asia like India and Pakistan. These
countries clearly do not belong to the early phase in the growth of the
money economy in our sense. In fact, outside the subsistence sectors

[1] United Nations Report on the *Enlargement of the Exchange Economy* (cited
above, p. 31), Tables 4 and 6, pp. 14–17 and passim.

they have a fairly complex economic and monetary structure. They also have more developed systems of transport and communications than many African countries. So, as I have suggested, the main reasons for their large subsistence sectors may be found in the over-crowding on land which has reduced the peasants to a minimum subsistence level, with no saleable surplus output to facilitate their entry into the money economy. In broad terms, therefore, we may distinguish two types of subsistence sector. The first type, charac-terizing most of the African peasant economies, is mainly caused by a lack of effective demand. The second type, characterized by the over-populated peasant economies of Asia, is mainly caused by a lack of supply.

The second phase in the growth of the money economy in our sense is represented by the more developed peasant export economies, such as Burma, Thailand and Ghana. These countries still have a sizeable subsistence sector (about a quarter of the total land and male labour employed in the case of Ghana), but a larger proportion of their peasants have been engaged in whole-time production for the export market for many decades and they have become fully com-mitted to the money economy. This dependence on the export mar-ket can be seen from the fact that during the Great Depression of 1931 and the decade which followed it, it was the peasants in these countries who seem to have suffered most from the fluctuations in the export market, and complained most about the monopoly power of the foreign export–import firms. It is also significant that in the post-war period, and after their independence, both Burma and Ghana took enthusiastically to the system of marketing boards for the peasant exports. Burma has frankly used this system to nationalize the foreign export–import firms which dominated her pre-war rice trade, and to obtain the revenue for financing her industrial develop-ment plans. Ghana's marketing board started with the official aim of stabilizing the peasants' incomes, but is tending towards the Burmese pattern, and becoming the chief source of revenue for economic development.

Peasant exports and economic development

There has been a considerable amount of controversy about how far the West African marketing boards have effectively stabilized peasant incomes, and how far the Burmese marketing board has exploited the peasants under the guise of protecting them from the middlemen. But beyond the problems of short-term economic stability and distribution of incomes, there is the long-term problem of how far the increase in peasant export production still offers a satisfactory basis for further economic development in these countries. A fuller answer to this question must wait until we consider the factors likely to affect the future trends in the world market demand for primary products in Chapter 9. But even at this stage it is possible to bring out a number of points which have emerged from our analysis of the supply side of the question.

I have shown that peasant export production expanded without the introduction of radical improvements in the agricultural techniques used in subsistence production, and that when the peasants took to 'specializing' in export crops it merely meant that they were devoting the whole of their resources to export production. In doing this they took full advantage of the *market opportunities* available to them; but this does not mean that they took full advantage of the *technical opportunities* to improve their productivity. Peasant holdings in rice production, for example, have remained approximately the same, and the same combination of land, labour and capital have been used throughout half a century of rapid expansion in rice exports from South-East Asia. The same thing is true of the West African cocoa exports. Although there are some large cocoa farmers with annual incomes above £500, on the whole the productivity of resources in the cocoa industry has remained constant.[1] This means that 'specialization' in these peasant export economies is not the same thing as 'specialization' as understood by Western economists who use the term to mean a greater degree of division of labour leading to higher productivity and economies of production. If this is true, then peasant export production continuing on the same basis as before is bound to come to a stop sooner or later, even if demand conditions continue to be favourable. Sooner or later the extension of cultivation will press against the limits of cultivable hinterland, and thereafter population growth will outstrip export expansion and lead to a situation of overpopulation and 'disguised unemployment' in agriculture.

Two very different policy conclusions can be drawn from this. The first is that peasant export expansion is not likely to offer a

[1] W. A. Lewis, *Report on the Industrialization of the Gold Coast*, Accra, 1953, p. 3. For other cases of decline in productivity in peasant agriculture due to use of less suitable land, over-cropping and soil erosion, see Ingram, op. cit., pp. 49–50, and the UN Report on the *Enlargement of the Exchange Economy* (cited above, p. 31), p. 22.

satisfactory basis for a continuous and self-sustained type of economic development, and that therefore these countries should turn to manufacturing industry. This is the conclusion favoured by many of the newly independent developing countries in South-East Asia and Africa, although they do not so far suffer from overpopulation. Thus, they tend to divert the larger part of the proceeds from peasant exports obtained through the marketing boards and other forms of taxation to industrial development, so starving the peasant export sector of capital and technical assistance.[1] But an entirely different policy conclusion can also be drawn. The fact that peasant export production has not shown any technical improvements in the past does not mean that it is inherently incapable of improvement if adequate resources are ploughed back into it. The past pattern merely shows that these opportunities for improvements have been neglected because, with unused land easily available, it was so much easier to expand along existing lines than to try to introduce improved methods of production. Further, in so far as the peasant export economies of South-East Asia and Africa have not yet reached a state of over-population in relation to land, it will be necessary for them to raise productivity in peasant production if only to release the labour required for their industrialization. These two conflicting policy conclusions will be considered in Chapter 9.

[1] An extreme case of this tendency was found until recently in the policy of the Burmese Government, which, like the Ghanaian Government, obtained on the average some 40% of its total revenue from the profits of the marketing board and other taxation on exports. Yet the only direct benefit which the Burmese peasants obtained from the earlier development plans were the subsidized agricultural loans which covered only about 16% of their total short-term credit requirements. cf. Aye Hlaing, *Some Aspects of Seasonal Agricultural Loans in Burma*, Rangoon 1958, pp. 3–5. See also Ghana's *Second Development Plan*, Accra 1959, p. 62.

4

MINES AND PLANTATIONS AND THE GROWTH

OF THE WAGE ECONOMY

Mines and plantations are large-scale enterprises which normally require more labour per unit of land than peasant agriculture. They generally created a very laige expansion in the demand for indigenous labour when they started their operations in the underdeveloped countries. This expansion in demand for labour could be met without difficulty in the countries which were already densely populated. But frequently the location of natural resources required the mines and plantations to be set up in countries which had sparse populations in relation to their available resources. Here we have an interesting situation which leads us straight into the fundamental issues of the development of the wage economy in the underdeveloped countries.

If we apply the ordinary demand and supply analysis to the labour market, we should expect to have a generally higher level of wages in sparsely populated countries than in densely populated countries. We should also expect the wage level to show a rising trend over a period of rapid expansion in output requiring more labour. These results are broadly borne out by experience in the newly settled regions of North America and Australia. But when we turn to the tropical underdeveloped countries which also started (in a lesser degree) with sparse populations in relation to the available land, these expected results failed to take place. Here the mine and plantation owners continually complained about 'labour shortage'. But the wages they paid in the sparsely populated countries were not noticeably higher than those they paid in the overpopulated countries. Moreover, these wages tended to stick at their initial level in spite of the rapid expansion in the production of the mining and plantation exports.

Origins of the 'cheap labour policy'

The owners of the mines and plantations usually explained this situation in terms of the very poor quality of labour they could recruit from the subsistence economies, whether densely or sparsely populated. According to them, (the uniformly low level of wages which prevailed in all types of underdeveloped countries merely reflected the uniformly low level of labour productivity in all these countries. Some would go on to contrast the poor quality of indigenous labour with the better quality of the European immigrant labour which flowed into North America and Australasia, and use this to explain the pattern of high wages and high productivity which developed in these newly settled regions. Some would complain that even at the low wages paid, the indigenous labour was 'expensive' because its productivity was lower still.

To these quantitative and qualitative factors, I should add a third set of factors which affected the type of wage economy which developed in the underdeveloped countries. These factors include the employers' conventional beliefs that, in general, indigenous labour not only had low productivity but had limited capacity for improvement; and that it was used to the customarily low material standard of living and would not respond positively to the incentive of higher wages. This crystallized into the convention of maintaining low wages in the underdeveloped countries which may be contrasted with the convention of maintaining high wages in the newly settled regions. As we shall see, in the formative stages of the wage economy, these conventional standards of wages could play an important part in influencing the future path of development.

Let us now consider how these three sets of factors acted on each other. The comparative productivity of indigenous labour in the mining and plantation sector and in the peasant sector was affected in two ways. In so far as the mining and plantation sector employed modern methods of production using a larger amount of capital per unit of labour, we should expect the productivity of indigenous labour to be higher here than in the peasant sector. If this were the only effect, we should expect the mines and plantations to be able to attract labour from the peasant sector by paying higher wages based on higher productivity. But unfortunately, in the early stages of entry into the wage economy, the quality of the raw indigenous labour just emerging out of the subsistence economy was undoubtedly very poor. It was unused to the industrial discipline of having to work

regularly and continuously at the new rhythm required by the productive organization of the mines and plantations. Frequently, it lacked
basic physical stamina because of malnutrition and disease. It therefore needed some time before it could efficiently perform even the
most unskilled of tasks, which confirmed the employers' beliefs about
the limited capacity of indigenous labour. Now, given these handi-
caps of rawness and inexperience, the productivity of indigenous
labour in the mining and plantation sector at the initial stage was not
only below its potential long-term level; it was sometimes not much
higher than its productivity in the peasant sector itself.

These transitional difficulties were not too serious in the overpopulated countries. Where the indigenous population was already
struggling at the minimum subsistence level, the mines and plantations could obtain an adequate supply of labour even at the wage
level fixed according to the low initial productivity of labour. But
in the sparsely populated countries where peasant agriculture offered
more attractive opportunities, the conflict between the quantitative
and qualitative aspects of the labour supply gave rise to a dilemma
with far-reaching consequences. (1) If the mines and plantations were
to fix wages according to the initial short-run productivity of the raw
labour, the wage level would be too low to attract a sufficient supply
of labour and they would suffer from a 'labour shortage'. (2) If they
were to raise wages, and succeeded in attracting a sufficient supply of
labour, they would suffer from having to pay the raw labour above its
initial short-run productivity during the transition period. At this
juncture, the third set of forces which I have described as the conventional standard of wages came into play, and the mines and
plantations opted for the policy of keeping wages low.

The far-reaching consequences of this decision can be seen by
contrasting the possible effects of the two alternatives. Had the mines
and plantations adopted the policy of raising wages to attract more
labour, the gap between the wages and the short-run productivity of
the raw labour would have induced them to adopt various further
policies of economizing labour and raising its productivity—say by
more careful selection, gradation and training, or by the introduction
of labour-saving methods such as a greater degree of mechanization.
As we shall see, it would not have been easy to pursue such a policy
in the setting of the underdeveloped countries, for there were further
complications arising out of the transition phase itself. But if they
had succeeded, then the mines and plantations would have performed
their expected role as the 'leading sector', raising productivity in the

rest of the economies in which they operated. As it was, their low wage policy induced them to use labour extravagantly, merely as an undifferentiated mass of 'cheap' or 'expendable' brawn-power. So through the vicious circle of low wages and low productivity, the productivity of the indigenous labour even in the sparsely populated countries was fossilized at its very low initial level.

This may be contrasted with the pattern of high wages and high productivity which developed in the newly settled regions of North America and Australasia. This difference cannot be explained simply in terms of the better quality of European immigrants into these regions. As Professor Taussig has pointed out, one of the reasons for the rapid development of mechanization in American industry was not the high quality but the *low* initial productivity of new European immigrants in juxtaposition with the convention of high wages which was already established in the United States, reflecting her sparse population relatively to her abundant natural resources. The desire to maintain the high American wage level in the face of fresh waves of immigrants from Europe was a strong inducement for the invention of machinery 'that will almost run itself. Here the new immigrant can be used. So far as the American can do this sort of machine-making to peculiar advantage, so far can he pay the immigrant on the higher American scale and yet hold his own against the European competitor who pays lower wages to the immigrant's stay-at-home fellow.'[1]

[1] F. W. Taussig, *Some Aspects of the Tariff Question*, Cambridge, Mass. 1931, p. 43. Taussig's analysis however brings out a serious limitation to the application of the American-type high-wage policy to the underdeveloped countries. Such a policy can be successfully maintained only if the employers are both willing and able to adopt new methods of production raising labour productivity to match high wages *without contracting the total volume of employment*. In recent times, many of the newly independent underdeveloped countries have in fact succeeded in pushing up wages in their modern mining and manufacturing sectors by using government and trade union pressure. But this has not been matched by their ability to create favourable economic conditions to enable the employers to raise labour productivity while expanding the volume of employment; and so raising wages above the free market level merely leads to an excessive substitution of capital for labour, allowing a minority of workers to earn high wages in the highly capital-intensive modern sector side by side with unemployment and low wages in the rest of the economy. Although the old cheap labour policy missed genuine opportunities to raise the productivity of indigenous labour in the underdeveloped countries, it does not follow that its productivity will be automatically raised simply by pushing up wages. cf. pp. 50–1 below.

Migrant labour and the partial entry into the wage economy

Let us now turn to the question of how the mines and plantations managed to obtain any labour at all in the sparsely populated countries when the wages they offered were not very much above, or might even be below, the real income which the indigenous people could obtain in the subsistence economy. One very important factor which facilitated this was the 'migrant labour' system which still prevails in most of the mining and plantation economies of Africa. This again is a peculiarity of the transition stage. In the peasant sector, we have seen that at the early stage of entry into the money economy, the peasants produced the cash crop on a spare-time basis while continuing to produce their subsistence requirements. The migrant labour system is a counterpart of that, representing a partial entry into the wage economy. Under this system, those who came to work in the mines and plantations still retained a foothold in the subsistence economy. They regarded their wage-earning activity not as a permanent full-time employment but as a periodical spare-time activity to earn a certain sum of money *in addition* to their claims on the subsistence economy. They were therefore quite willing to accept the low wages offered by the mines and plantations since these were regarded not as full compensation for the alternative economic opportunities (which were not sacrificed) but merely as an additional source of income. But precisely because of this reason, the migrant labour normally returned to their families in the subsistence sector after having worked a certain period and having earned a certain target sum of money. They were then replaced by a fresh batch of recruits who in their turn worked and returned home.

In spite of its obvious short-term advantages, the migrant labour system reinforced the pattern of low wages and low productivity in a number of ways. With the high rate of labour turnover associated with the migrant labour system, it was not possible or worthwhile to select and train indigenous labour for skilled work, even if the mines and plantations were willing to do it. The same person did not stay on the job long enough for the purpose, and the labour supply remained a succession of raw recruits. But on the other hand, the migrant labour system provided the mines and plantations with a very convenient stream of casual labour for which they did not need to take much care and responsibility. Most of the workers were adult single males who had left (or were encouraged to leave) their families behind in the subsistence economy. So the mines and plantations did not feel obliged to pay wages sufficient to maintain the worker and his family or to invest in housing and other welfare projects to enable him to settle permanently with his family on the location of his work. Further, during the slumps in the export market, the redundant labour could be laid off and returned to the subsistence sector without continuing responsibility for them. We can now see why, having once started on the migrant labour system, the mines and plantations tried to perpetuate it as long as possible. The switch-over from a low-wage, low productivity pattern to a high-wage, high productivity pattern would involve not merely raising wages, but also the very heavy expenses and responsibilities of converting a casual labour force into a stabilized labour force on a permanent basis. One should also take into account the fact that investment flowed into the mines and plantations under the stimulus of shortages of their products and the high prices paid for them. They were therefore under continual pressure to take advantage of favourable market conditions which might change quickly. During the booms, therefore, output had to be expanded as quickly as possible along the line of least resistance, and there was no time to wait for the fruits of a longer-term labour policy. During the slumps, no capital could be attracted to inaugurate such a policy.

The migrant labour system also strengthened the employers' belief that the indigenous people were not only content to accept low wages but did not respond positively to economic incentives. This was supposed to be 'proved' by the fact that the migrant workers who usually came to work to earn a fixed target sum of money (to meet their marriage expenses, for example) could be made to work for a longer period when the wage rate was reduced. But this reaction could also be induced from workers in the advanced countries provided the employers could press down the wage rate without restraint from the trade unions or public opinion. The real point, therefore, is whether the wants of the indigenous people were so limited that they would prefer not to earn above a certain sum; that is to say, whether the target sum they set out to earn was not merely a minimum but also a maximum target. Now, it may frequently happen that in the short run, given a sudden and transient rise in wage rates, the supply of indigenous labour would contract. But as we have seen from the behaviour of peasant producers, the indigenous people responded very vigorously to sustained positive economic incentives over the long period during which new wants and luxuries became semi-necessities. It is difficult, therefore, to accept this doctrine of the 'backward-bending' supply curve of labour in the underdeveloped countries without further evidence that a systematic application of wage incentives in favour of extra work, such as bonuses and overtime payments, had failed to induce a greater supply of labour over the long run.

Whatever its weaknesses, the doctrine of the 'backward-bending' supply curve of labour was used to rationalize the policy of using negative pressures to squeeze more labour out of the subsistence economy when the voluntary supply of migrant labour became inadequate for the expanding demand of the mines and plantations. Sometimes the pressure was applied directly, and the administrative power of the colonial government or indigenous rulers was used to direct labour into the mines and plantations. More frequently, the pressure was applied indirectly, by imposing a poll tax or a hut tax which obliged the indigenous people in the subsistence economy to come out and work in the mines and plantations so that they could pay their taxes.

Until recently, the mines and plantations in most African countries have been able to obtain the bulk of their labour requirements on the basis of the migrant labour system, reinforced by taxation and administrative pressures. The alternative economic opportunities offered by peasant cash production have not been able to break the mould of the cheap labour policy. They merely regulated the labour supply from different regions—regions with prosperous peasant agriculture sending relatively little labour, and regions with little or no peasant cash crops supplying the bulk of labour for the mines and plantations.[1] But as we shall see, the economic power of the mines and plantations which has withstood the economic pressures from the peasant sector is now yielding to the political pressure of economic nationalism and trade unions in some of the newly independent African countries.

Immigrant labour

In other underdeveloped countries, such as Malaya and Ceylon, where migrant labour of the African type was not available on a sufficient scale, or where the development of peasant cash crops made taxation an ineffective method of increasing the supply of labour to the mines and plantations, a different solution was adopted. This was to import immigrant labour systematically and on a large scale

[1] See the UN Report on the *Enlargement of the Exchange Economy in Tropical Africa*, New York 1954, Tables 9 and 10, and also W. J. Barber, *The Economy of British Central Africa*, London 1961, chs. 8 and 9.

from the overpopulated countries of India and China. The method of obtaining 'indentured' labour from India under which the employers agreed to pay the passage of the immigrant workers in return for an agreement to work a certain number of years for a certain wage rate was first adopted in the sugar plantations of the West Indies after the emancipation of the slave labour. After that, it spread not only to the countries of South-East Asia, but also to places such as Fiji, Mauritius, or East and Central Africa. Indeed the immigrant labour from India and China was recruited on so large a scale that it has been said that these two countries, together with Britain, were the 'three mother countries' of the British Empire.[1]

Both migrant and immigrant labour involved movements of labour across national boundaries into the underdeveloped countries where the mines and plantations were located. The difference is that whereas the African type of migrant worker accepted the low wages offered by the mines and plantations as an addition to his income from the subsistence economy, the Indian and the Chinese immigrants accepted them because they could not find work even at these low wages in the overpopulated countries from which they came. In their case, however, the effect was to depress the wage level in the thinly populated underdeveloped countries to that of the overpopulated countries. Without appreciably relieving the population pressure in India and China, the outflow of cheap labour from these countries created serious problems for the underdeveloped countries which received it. In many of these countries, the Indian and Chinese labour came to form a considerable proportion of the total population, and frequently had a faster rate of growth than the indigenous population. When the indigenous population itself began to grow, therefore, the problem of population pressure was aggravated. Further, particularly in the South-East Asian countries, the presence of large Indian or Chinese minorities has created the complex socio-economic problems of the 'plural society' which frequently overshadow the problem of economic development itself.

Mines and plantations and economic development

In recent times, it has become fashionable to look upon the mines and plantations as 'foreign enclaves' which are incapable of transmitting a satisfactory type of economic growth to the developing countries.

[1] L. C. Knowles, *The Economic Development of the British Overseas Empire*, London 1928–36, vol. I, pp. viii and 182–201.

The critics tend to put most of the blame on the fact that they are concerned with primary production and not with manufacturing industry. Our analysis has, however, suggested that the failure of the mines and plantations to become the 'leading sector' in the under-developed countries was due, not to their producing primary exports as such, but to their cheap labour policy which has perpetuated the pattern of low wages and low productivity. With the system of using indigenous labour mainly as an undifferentiated mass of brawn-power, it is not surprising that Adam Smith's vision of the growth of the exchange economy and the division of labour 'improving the skill and dexterity of the people' should remain largely unfulfilled. The 'dualism' between foreign technology and management in the mines and plantations representing the 'modern' sector, and the rest of the economy representing the traditional sector has persisted.

If the mines and plantations did little to raise the technical efficiency of the indigenous people, how far have they extended the people's purely market opportunities? In many African mining economies, the existence of a large number of wage earners has created regular markets for staple food produced by indigenous cultivators.[1] The wage income from the mines and plantations has the same effect in spreading the money economy as the cash income from peasant production. But even here there is a snag. We have seen that the money economy cannot spread fully in the peasant sector until the peasants have switched over from part-time to full-time production of cash crops, buying their food requirements from other farmers. Similarly, the wages paid out by the mines and plantations cannot give rise to the full extent of secondary rounds of economic activity without further specialization. That is to say, the migrant labour force with one foot in the wage economy and another in the subsis-tence economy has to develop into two specialized groups, one con-sisting of a permanent stabilized body of full-time wage earners and the other specializing in full-time production of the cash crops. But while the peasant producer can assume full-time status by expanding his output while accepting the same market price per unit of his output, the migrant labourer cannot turn himself into a full-time wage employee so easily. His wages already represent full-time

[1] UN Report on the *Enlargement of the Exchange Economy* (cited above p. 31), pp. 32-3; cf. however Barber, op. cit., pp. 183-4 on the limitations on the market opportunities of the indigenous cultivators either because some plantations grow the food for their labour or because the mines purchase it from the European settler farmers.

work during the short periods for which he has taken up employment. The total earnings required to support himself and his family after they have become 'detribalized' without any further claim on the subsistence economy can therefore be met only by raising the wage per unit of his labour. On the other hand, for the mines and plantations, this switch-over means not merely raising wage rates, but also incurring the very heavy expenses in housing and welfare projects, and all the responsibilities of turning a casual labour force into a stabilized labour force.

But before they have been able to complete the process of transition from the migrant labour system to a modern wage economy into which the mass of their working population has been absorbed as a stabilized force, the newly independent African countries have been caught up by the new forces of economic nationalism and trade unionism. In a very short time, these forces have dramatically reversed the situation, particularly in the more prosperous mining economies such as Northern Rhodesia, now Zambia. Now instead of being held down by the monopoly power of the mines as employers, African wages are being rapidly pushed up far above the free market level by the trade unions and the governments. But this has not been matched by the capacity to create economic conditions in which productivity of African labour is raised to match the higher wages, without contracting the total volume of employment.[1] The net effect of the new wage policy is to induce an excessive substitution of capital for African labour in the mining sector, enabling a minority of African workers to enjoy the high wages from the highly capital-intensive methods of production while the non-unionized labour in the rest of the economy continues to suffer from unemployment and low wages. From the standpoint of longer-run economic development, the situation is worse than before. For, under the pressure of

[1] In the case of Northern Rhodesian copper mining, Professor Robert E. Baldwin has estimated that 'if the same ratio of African labour to copper output prevailed in 1959 as in 1949, African employment in the industry would have been 69,000 instead of 35,000'. Ironically enough, the existence of a powerful trade union of skilled European workers, earning some 15 to 20 times more than the African workers, has facilitated the rapid rise of African wages since 1953. Both the African trade unions and the government accepted the mono-polistically determined European wage level and then pushed up the wages of unskilled African workers towards this high level on grounds of fairness and equity. R. E. Baldwin, 'A study in dual economy—the case of copper mining in Northern Rhodesia', *Race*, November 1962. For another example of the 'dual' wage structure, this time in Venezuela, see D. Seers, 'The mechanism of an open petroleum economy', *Social and Economic Studies*, March 1964.

trade unions and the government combined with 'sympathetic rise in wages', the higher wave level of the mines spreads to the other parts of the modern sector, such as the railways, the government and manufacturing industry where the productivity of labour is lower than in the mining sector. Thus, before they have completed the process of absorbing the labour from the subsistence sector into a fully fledged wage economy, many countries in Africa and in Latin America find themselves saddled in their modern industrial sector with wage scales which are too high and methods of production which are too capital-intensive. This tends not only to aggravate the dualism between the modern and traditional sectors, but also to inhibit the growth of an industrial sector which can stand up to international competition from other countries where the wage levels are better adjusted to the levels of labour productivity.

How far can the mines and plantations contribute to the future growth of the developing countries? Here, as in the previous chapter, I shall defer consideration of the factors which may affect the future world market demand for these primary exports to Chapter 9 and concentrate on the points which have so far emerged on the supply side of the question. It seems that in the context of many newly independent countries, there are two formidable obstacles which can prevent the foreign-owned mines and plantations from making their full potential contribution to economic development.

The first is the wholesale reaction against primary production and in favour of manufacturing industries on the part of the new independent countries, even where there is no serious population pressure and 'disguised unemployment'. Our analysis suggests that the failure of the mines and plantations to become the 'leading sector' in the underdeveloped countries is due, not to their producing primary exports as such, but to their inappropriate wage policies. In the old days, it was the cheap labour policy which moulded the pattern of low wages and low productivity. Nowadays, there is increasing danger that economic development may be inhibited by the opposite mistake of pushing up the wages of the minority of workers employed in the modern mining and industrial sector too high through the pressure of trade unions and the government. The experiences of the Latin American countries, where the process of expanding domestic manufacturing industry to substitute imports has been jeopardized by this kind of 'dualism', serves to confirm the belief that the failure of the modern sector to transmit growth to the rest of the economy arises from deeper causes than the simple contrast between primary production and manufacturing industry.[1]

The second obstacle is the rising tide of economic nationalism in the underdeveloped countries. The reaction against the past colonial pattern tends to be even stronger in the mining and plantation economies than in the peasant export economies since economic nationalism is reinforced by the conventional conflict between indigenous labour and foreign capital. In extreme cases, there has been outright nationalization of all foreign-owned enterprises. More generally, there has been an insistence on obtaining a larger share of their profits through higher taxation and royalties, and a larger share of the management through requiring a larger number of indigenous personnel in skilled and managerial grades: these, in addition to the substantial wage increases we have considered. The question is how far these policies, which are primarily designed to get a larger share of the existing cake for the nationals of the underdeveloped countries, are compatible with the development policy of trying to increase and maintain the expansion in the total size of the cake. In many under-developed countries, foreign-owned mining concerns are the principal source, not only of government revenues but also of the foreign exchange earnings which are badly needed to pay for the imported capital goods and materials required for the development pro-grammes. Thus it is a matter of great importance and delicate judg-ment for the governments of these countries to extract the maximum revenue from these foreign companies without discouraging them from further expansion in investment and output which would have serious repercussions on future economic development.

The potential contribution of the foreign enterprises to the developing countries is not confined to the supply of capital and foreign exchange. From a longer-run point of view, it is more important to take into account the new ideas, technical skills and knowledge they can bring into these countries. Such skills and knowledge, developed in an articulated form and embodied in a going concern adjusted to local economic conditions cannot be replaced by technical aid programmes administered by a foot-loose group of foreign experts on short-term contracts. But the foreign enterprises cannot perform this 'educative' function and fulfil their role as a 'leading sector' diffusing modern technology and skills to the rest of the economy unless they are willing and able to undertake

[1] cf. for instance, Celso Furtado, 'Political obstacles to economic growth in Brazil', *International Affairs*, April 1965.

substantial investments both in material and human capital to raise
the efficiency of local labour in the context of an expanding volume of
total employment. Here, apart from the problem of the 'dualistic'
wage structure, the foreign concerns are naturally unwilling to undertake such slow-yielding types of investment unless they can be
reasonably sure of reaping the fruits of such policies in the long run.
But unfortunately, in the typical conditions of the newly independent
countries, this sense of security and inducement to wait for the fruits
of long-term policy is precisely what is not available to the foreign-
owned enterprises. This undoubtedly prevents them from making
their full potential contribution to the economic growth of the
developing countries.

5

FINANCIAL DUALISM AND MONETARY

DEPENDENCE AND INDEPENDENCE

Capital supply in the peasant sector

In the subsistence economy, each social unit such as the family or the village not only produces what it requires but also supplies its own productive resources, including capital. Saving mainly takes the form of an addition to the 'subsistence fund', enabling it to maintain a larger number of workers, or the same number of workers for a longer time. Given this, investment in durable capital can take place in various forms, such as the clearing of additional land for cultivation, or the construction of implements, irrigation works, public or private buildings. As we have seen, in the first phase of the money economy, the peasants produced the cash crop for export on a part-time basis while continuing to produce their subsistence crop. The expansion of peasant export production in this phase, therefore, was mainly 'self-financing'.

The spread of the money economy into the market for commodities and the improvement in transport and communications by themselves tend to economize the stocks of goods or the 'subsistence fund' which an underdeveloped society needs to carry itself on between one harvest and another. While each family unit had previously to carry its own stocks for emergency, now the function of carrying them in a pool for a larger number of family units is taken over by the village shop. Similarly, the effect of the spread of trade and communications in preventing local famines illustrates this economizing of reserve stocks of goods.

But the expansion of world demand for peasant exports required a quicker rate of new investment in the clearing of land than an individual family could usually finance out of its own savings and, with greater specialization, many families now switched over to a full-time production of the export crop, buying their food and other requirements. Even in this second stage, peasant producers could be self-financing provided they saved enough out of their proceeds from the cash crop. But in the majority of cases this did not happen, partly because of a high propensity to spend on imported goods and partly because of inexperience with a highly unstable export market which made peasant producers believe that the high prices of the good years would continue in the future. Lured by these optimistic expectations, they tended to borrow heavily to extend cultivation and to get into debt when prices came down.

Now the main source from which the peasants could borrow were and still are the 'non-institutional' lenders, such as the village money-lender, the landlord or the shopkeeper. The interest rates charged on these loans are usually very high.[1] The main reason for this is a real shortage of savings, but there are many important contributory factors arising out of imperfections in the market for borrowing and lending in the peasant sector. Considering the substantial amount of saving in this sector which still remains locked up in hoarded gold and jewellery, there seems to be scope for the introduction of a more efficient class of financial intermediaries which could bring down the interest rates to some extent. But so far little progress has been made in this direction. The Western commercial banks have offered little competition to the money-lenders because these banks are, so to speak, wholesalers dealing with larger amounts of loan, whereas the peasants require an efficient retail distribution of credit. On the other hand, it is widely believed that the money-lenders, the village shop-keepers and the landlords occupying strategic positions in the local economy can make use of their monopolistic powers over the peasants by charging excessively high rates of interest. We shall return to this point later on.

Financial dualism: old and new

The underdevelopment of the unorganized money market in the traditional peasant sector offers a striking contrast with the low interest rates and abundant credit facilities available in the organized

---

[1] A recent study has estimated that they range on the average between 24% and 36% per annum. The institutional lenders such as the cooperative societies are still generally inadequate, although in some cases, such as in West Africa, big export–import firms give considerable advances to the peasants through pro-duce buyers. (U Tun Wai, Interest Rates Outside the Organized Money Markets, *IMF Staff Papers*, November 1957.)

money market in the modern sector of the underdeveloped countries. This sector consists of the big foreign-owned enterprises in the export industries, the government and, more recently, the larger-scale modern manufacturing enterprises. The dualism in economic organization and production methods between the peasant sector and the mining–plantation sector is paralleled by the financial dualism between the traditional and the modern sectors. There are two distinct phases in financial dualism. The first, which represents the earlier phase in the development of domestic financial institutions, can be most clearly seen in the colonial economic setting with the modern sector oriented towards export production. The second is a more recent outcome of the policies to expand the modern manufacturing sector oriented towards the domestic market which most underdeveloped countries have adopted as a reaction against the older colonial economic pattern.

In the older economic setting the big foreign trading enterprises, mines and plantations, can raise their long-term capital at low rates of interest from the world capital markets. They can also borrow their short-term capital requirements cheaply from the commercial banks which are themselves branches of the banks located in the world financial centres. During the colonial period, one of the duties of the metropolitan power was to introduce the governments of the underdeveloped countries to the world capital market (a function now taken over by the World Bank). During that period, therefore, the governments also could raise their long-term capital cheaply from the world capital market. Apart from their imperial connection, one of the reasons why colonial governments in the pre-war days could usually borrow more cheaply than can the governments of the independent underdeveloped countries was the stability of the colonial type currency which precluded inflationary developments of the sort experienced by Japan and still being experienced in some of the Latin American countries.

The contrast between the high rates of interest and the small amount of capital used per unit of labour in the peasant sector and the low rates of interest and the capital-intensive methods of production in the mining and plantation sector has attracted criticism. It has been argued that the colonial governments deliberately neglected the development of peasant agriculture and the domestic manufacturing industry by diverting too much of the available capital funds into the mining and plantation sector. But this criticism is somewhat misdirected. The colonial governments had no choice of reallocating the capital supply to the peasant sector since, typically, private foreign investment flowed into the underdeveloped countries for the specific purpose of investment in the mining and plantation sector in response to favourable world market prices for particular commodities which that sector could produce. The only choice presented was having private investment in the mining and planta- tion sector or not having any private investment at all. The colonial governments generally encouraged this type of investment as they derived a considerable part of the total revenues from taxation and royalties on exports. Whether they should have used a greater part of these revenues for the encouragement of peasant agriculture is a more arguable matter and here judgments can differ. Further, the colonial governments would have found it difficult to attract private foreign investment into the domestic manufacturing sector. The size of the domestic markets for manufactured goods was generally too small to attract private foreign investment in the free-trade and open economy setting of the colonial era.

On the other hand, it is true to say that the operations of the Western commercial banks did not usually extend beyond short- term loans to big foreign-owned enterprises in the export sector. The banks frequently adopted rigid and conservative rules of credit- worthiness which few of the indigenous businessmen could satisfy.[1] Frequently the operations of the banks resulted in 'perverse' flows of credit, i.e. instead of channelling the funds from the world financial centres to the underdeveloped countries, some part of the local savings might be collected and lent to the world financial centres.[2] Thus the advantages which the peoples of the colonial countries obtained from the great financial centres in the metropolitan coun- tries should not be exaggerated. Directly, in their role as peasants, small traders, handicraft producers, they obtained little or no benefit. Only indirectly, mainly through government investment in transport and communications, could they count their benefits.

Nowadays, in most underdeveloped countries, the old financial dualism associated with the colonial type of monetary system has been overlaid and aggravated by the new financial dualism which has

---

[1] P. T. Bauer, *West African Trade*, London 1963, ch. 13, section 5.
[2] It has been estimated that between 1954 and 1959, some 20% to 30% of the funds collected by the banks in the British colonial territories were remitted out of these territories, almost wholly to the London head offices or money market. See E. Nevin, *Capital Funds in Underdeveloped Countries*, London, 1961, pp. 50–1.

developed since the attainment of monetary independence. In order to provide the background for this development, it is necessary to examine the change-over from monetary dependence to monetary independence.

The dependent monetary system

The monetary system which used to prevail in most Asian and African countries was a colonial type of monetary system, typified by the sterling exchange standard. Under this system, the currency of a colony was freely convertible at a fixed rate of exchange with sterling. It was issued by a currency board located in London and the issue was generally backed by 100% sterling reserves contributed out of the export earnings of the colony. The currency board was required to invest its reserve fund outside the colony, in British or other Commonwealth Government securities, although the colony received its share of the currency board profits. In effect, the colony was obliged to lend its monetary reserve funds to other countries in the Commonwealth. In line with the general reaction against the colonial economic pattern, this system has been criticized as being too rigid to provide adequately for the financial requirements of a developing country. I shall therefore briefly outline its working and contrast it later with the working of an independent monetary system.

The working of the 100% sterling exchange system in its pure form may be illustrated in terms of my model of the two stages in the growth of the money economy in a peasant export economy. In the first stage, the peasants produced the export crop only on a part-time basis while continuing to produce their subsistence requirements. Since they were self-sufficient in respect to locally produced food-stuffs and other goods, they had no need to hold cash for local transactions. Since their sole reason for producing the export crop was to obtain purchasing power over imports, we may assume that they spent the whole of their cash earnings on imported goods. At this stage, the money which flowed into the country to pay for the peasants' exports would flow out again immediately to pay for their imports. No 'localized' currency would be retained for long within the country. The function of money was merely to facilitate the barter between the exports and imports at agreed rates and a separate local currency was hardly needed. As a matter of fact, in the earlier phases of trade in West Africa, British silver coins were extensively used for this purpose.

In the second stage, the money economy has spread from foreign trade to domestic trade. Some of the peasants now devote all their resources to export production and no longer produce their subsistence requirements of foodstuffs and local commodities. So instead of spending the whole of their money income on imports only, they will spend a part of it on locally produced goods and services. What is more, since money transactions have now become more frequent, they will need to hold a certain amount of cash for carrying on their normal transactions.

They may also save and hoard money as a store of value for future needs. Similarly, those who receive the money payments from export producers in subsequent rounds of buying and selling will spend a part of their income on imports and a part of it on locally produced goods. They will also hold a certain amount of cash for normal transactions and saving. So of the total amount of money which has flowed into the country to pay for the peasants' exports, the part which has not flowed out again to pay for the imported goods purchased by the peasant exporters and by all those who receive money payments from them will be retained inside the country as 'localized' currency. The amount of the localized currency is equal to the peasant producers' total earnings from export minus total spending on imports by themselves and all others who receive money payments from them. This surplus of earnings over expenditure by the residents of the country in terms of the foreign currency contributes to the 100% sterling reserve for the localized currency. This result follows because the country in my example has no other means of acquiring its supply of money except through its exports.

I have said that the amount of the localized currency is equal to 'the surplus of earnings over expenditure in terms of the foreign currency by the residents of the country' and have used this clumsy phrase deliberately to distinguish it from the geographical export surplus in the usual sense as shown by the trade figures. In my example, even if the country has no other source of export than the peasant exports, the geographical export surplus will be different from the relevant surplus in our sense. For the geographical export surplus will include payments to the non-residents such as the profit remittances of the foreign export–import firms. What is relevant for our present purpose is the surplus earning of foreign exchange accruing to the residents of the country; they could have imported consumers' or capital goods but have preferred to pass it on to the currency board because they wish to hold their assets in the form of local currency.

I can now easily extend the analysis to determine the amount of the localized currency for a more general type of economy whose exports originate not only from the peasant sector but also from the plantation and mining sector. In this case the export earners will include not only peasant producers but all other resident wage earners in the mines and plantations and other auxiliary export industries such as transport and processing. We should also remember that the amount of localized currency existing at a given time within a country is an accumulated stock; the surplus foreign exchange earnings of the residents each year add to the stock and the deficit foreign exchange expenditure of the residents subtract from it.

Monetary independence

In the post-war years, with the attainment of political independence, the developing countries of Asia and Africa have also asserted their monetary independence by establishing their own central banks. The Latin American countries did this in the 1920s or 1930s, and India and Thailand also have central banks dating from that period. The external limit to the currency issue is removed and the governments of these countries can now borrow from the central banks to meet their budget deficits. The newly established central banks, however, do not have the power, which their counterparts in the advanced countries have, to control the commercial banks through traditional methods such as changing the central bank rate or varying the supply of money by buying or selling securities in the open market. For one thing, the stock exchange and the money market in these countries are too underdeveloped for this purpose. For another, the foreign commercial banks look upon their headquarters in London or elsewhere and not upon the local central bank as their 'lender of the last resort'. To make up for this, the central banks in many countries have been granted extensive legal powers over the commercial banks, ranging from requirements to hold certain minimum proportions of their funds with the central banks, to more detailed controls over their rates of interest, the amount and direction of their lending and other 'selective controls'.[1]

[1] U Tun Wai, Interest Rates in the Organized Money Markets of Underdeveloped Countries. *IMF Staff Papers*, August 1956, pp. 258–62; E. Nevin, op. cit., ch. 2; and A. K. Cairncross, *Factors in Economic Development*, London 1962, ch. 10.

Finally, in addition to the central banks, many government 'development banks' have been set up to finance domestic industry and agriculture.

Under the old sterling exchange type of monetary system, inflation was avoided by a control over the currency issue combined with the tradition of a balanced budget. Further, the automatic convertibility between the local currency and sterling eliminated balance of payments disequilibrium. Thus when a country had an excess of imports over exports, an equivalent amount of local currency was converted into sterling to pay for the deficit, and the reduction of the local money supply reduced the incomes until imports were equated to exports at a lower equilibrium level. With the attainment of monetary independence, however, most of the developing countries have suffered from varying degrees of inflation, and some of the more extreme cases are to be found in Latin America. Further, owing to various factors such as the decline in foreign exchange reserves, balance-of-payments pressure and a general decline in confidence aggravated in many cases by political instability, the external values of the currencies of the developing countries have generally fallen below the official rates of exchange, setting up pressures for one-way conversion of the local currency into a more stable international currency. The developing countries are, however, unwilling to lower their official rates of exchange to the free market level, either because they wish to avoid a worsening in the terms of trade between their exports and their imports or because they fear that, once they start devaluing their currency, they may be caught in a cumulative spiral of inflation and devaluation. They have, therefore, concentrated mainly on tightening their controls on foreign exchange and imports, using quantitative controls of varying complexity and severity. How far do these changes help the economic development of these countries in so far as it can be influenced by monetary and financial factors?

There are three possible advantages which may be claimed for an independent monetary system.

First, under the old system the fluctuations in incomes of the underdeveloped countries caused by the export booms and slumps tended to be magnified through the free operation of commercial banks. Commercial banks tend to expand credit during the booms because their cash reserves have increased, and contract lending during the slumps, aggravating the fall in incomes. So, in theory at least, there is a good case for the central bank to pursue a contra-cyclical policy of moderating the expansion in incomes during the boom and adding to its foreign exchange reserves, and moderating the fall in income during the slump and releasing foreign exchange to pay for the excess imports which would follow from such a policy. But, in practice, this can be done only if the central bank can stock up foreign exchange during a boom. Unfortunately, with the upward surge of government expenditure during a boom (such as the Korean boom), the central bank has not usually been able to accumulate enough foreign exchange reserves to pursue such a policy.

Secondly, now that the central bank can increase the supply of money without having to acquire an equivalent amount of foreign exchange, and without having to invest a large part of it outside the country, it may be able to release some funds for domestic long-term investment out of its currency reserves. When the central bank first took over the reserves from the currency board, the release of funds for this purpose was sometimes quite substantial, but it was a once-for-all transfer. How far the central bank can release funds for domestic investment on a continuing basis depends on how seriously it takes its duty of maintaining the external value of the currency. If, for instance, it wishes to achieve the same degree of stability of the external value of the currency as under the old system, it cannot hope to economize its reserves very much to release funds for other purposes. One of the hard facts of life is that the external world tends to have more confidence, other things being equal, in a national currency which is freely convertible into a well-established international currency than in one which is not convertible.

The third possible advantage which may be claimed for an independent monetary system is of course that of deficit financing for economic development. I shall have more to say about this subject later on, in Chapter 8; for the moment only one point need be made. Deficit financing was originally advocated to deal with a situation of depression in the advanced countries. Now this situation differs from that of the underdeveloped countries in that in the advanced countries both unemployed labour and all the productive capacity which goes with it are readily available and can be made to increase output in a short time. By contrast, in the underdeveloped countries we either have unemployed labour without other productive re-sources, as in the overpopulated countries, or under-utilized land, labour and savings which are the result of market imperfections, incomplete growth of the exchange economy and other *structural* defects of the economic system. Unlike the unemployed resources of the advanced countries in a depression, the potentially available resources of the underdeveloped countries have to be mobilized over a long period, mainly by correcting the structural defects which have given rise to them. The level of output in the advanced countries in a depression can be raised by expanding the aggregate amount of effective demand, but the expansion of output in the underdeveloped countries depends more on the way in which the extra funds are injected into particular parts of the economy than merely on the aggregate of the amount of funds that deficit financing creates.

In many underdeveloped countries, the theoretical advantages of an independent monetary system have been frequently outweighed by the practical consequences of the freedom to pursue inappropriate fiscal and monetary policies.

Some of the critics of the old monetary system have argued that while monetary stability was indispensable in the days when economic development was left to foreign private enterprise, it is no longer of vital importance at the present time. The governments of the developing countries have taken over the function of economic development, and an increasing amount of external capital flows through international or intergovernmental channels. While this argument has some force, it seriously underrates the consequences of monetary instability on the domestic private sector of the underdeveloped countries. It should be remembered that many underdeveloped countries, notably in Africa, are still in the early stages of development of the money economy, with the larger part of their productive resources in the subsistence sector. Further, in almost all underdeveloped countries, the exchange economy has yet to spread from the market for commodities to the market for factors of production, particularly towards a more developed wage economy and capital market. This however, requires not only a wider use of money as a medium of exchange, but also developing the habit of using money as a 'unit of account' for more rational allocation of resources, and what is more important for our present purpose, using money as a 'store of value' for economic assets. On the other hand, with monetary policies which induce a distrust in the use of money as a unit of account and a flight from money as a store of value, it is difficult to see how the domestic resources of the underdeveloped countries can be effectively mobilized by a more comprehensive growth of the money economy.

The new dualism

The most serious consequences of the new-style fiscal and monetary policies are to be found in the aggravation of the economic dualism between the modern industrial sector and the traditional sector. This is generally true for all underdeveloped countries seeking to promote domestic industrialization in the characteristic conditions of domestic inflation and balance-of-payments difficulties, irrespective of the degree of population pressure on their natural resources. The peasants, the small traders and craftsmen in the traditional sector have always suffered from a shortage of capital and high rates of interest because of the much higher risks and costs of lending money on a retail basis to these classes of small borrower. But now, this handicap has been aggravated by government policies to promote domestic industrialization. These policies have the effect of providing the scarce capital and foreign exchange resources and public economic services on excessively favourable terms to the larger economic units in the modern sector and on excessively unfavourable terms to the small economic units in the traditional sector.

The larger economic units can borrow on favourable terms, since many underdeveloped countries have pursued a 'cheap money' policy and the central banks of the capital-scarce countries such as India and Pakistan, have consistently maintained an artificially low level of interest rates—lower than the prevailing rates in the capital-abundant developed countries during much of the post-war period. This has the effect of inhibiting the flow of outside commercial capital funds into the underdeveloped countries. In many cases this inflow has already been reduced by increasing foreign exchange controls on the operations of foreign commercial banks which in some countries have been nationalized. The artificially low rates of interest which are frequently below the rate of the decline in the value of money through inflation also have the effect of discouraging saving and creating an excess demand for loans. The channelling of the bulk of the domestic savings at low rates of interest to the modern industrial sector means a reduction in the supply of capital and higher rates of interest for peasant agriculture and other small economic units in the traditional sector.

Similarly, the apparatus of foreign exchange and import controls set up to alleviate the balance-of-payments difficulties has also been used to discriminate in favour of the modern manufacturing sector and against the traditional sector. The modern sector is usually allocated the lion's share of the available foreign exchange and the manufacturing industries are encouraged to adopt excessively capital-intensive methods of production because the imported capital goods are obtainable cheaply at the over-valued exchange rates and there is a strong incentive to substitute these cheap imported capital goods for labour.

The peasant farmers and the small economic units suffer from the import and the foreign exchange controls firstly because of the rise in the price of the imported consumers' goods and secondly because of the difficulties of obtaining the foreign exchange and import permits for the imports they require. The small economic units in the traditional sector are simply not equipped to cope with the complexities of the red tape involved in trying to obtain the necessary official permits. This has a more damaging effect on economic development than is generally appreciated. In many peasant export economies, particularly in Africa, imports of cheap consumers' goods still play a vital role as incentive goods in stimulating the expansion of export production and the growth of a money economy. Elsewhere, the imported inputs such as chemical fertilizer or yarn and dye stuffs have come to play an increasingly important part for the small economic units in the traditional sector.

On top of all this, the traditional sector suffers from the unequal distribution of government expenditure on public services between the urban centres and the rural districts. In particular, public services such as transport and communications and electric power are generally more readily available and on more favourable terms to the large economic units in the modern sector than to the small economic units in the traditional sector.

The governments in some of the underdeveloped countries have tried to improve the credit conditions in the traditional sector by passing usury laws and by the setting up of government agricultural banks and cooperative credit societies. The usury laws controlling the rates of interest which the money-lenders can charge the small borrowers have proved to be abortive since they do not take into account the real economic factors behind the high rates of interest in the traditional sector, viz. the overall scarcity of capital funds plus the extra risks and costs of lending money to a large number of small borrowers. In spite of the widely held belief that the money-lenders, the middlemen and the landlords charge exploitatively high rates of interest, the government-sponsored agencies have rarely been able to provide the marketing and credit facilities required by the peasants as cheaply and effectively as the existing middlemen and money-lenders. For one thing, the local traders and money-lenders have much lower overhead costs than the numerous branches which a central agency would have to open to deal directly with a large number of peasants dispersed throughout the countryside. For another, the money-lenders and middlemen can make quick and flexible decisions in the light of the local market conditions, whereas the coordination of the decisions between the central agency and its local branches has to be carried out by administrative rules and procedures which tend to be rigid, cumbersome and unadaptable to local conditions. Given these difficulties, the government efforts to improve the credit facilities in the traditional sector tend to take the form of supplying a limited amount of subsidized loans through the cooperative societies to some highly favoured 'model villages'. These seemingly impressive 'show pieces' however have no effect on lowering the high rates of interest which prevail in the rest of the traditional sector.

If this analysis is accepted, two main types of policies are suggested for the reduction of financial dualism in the underdeveloped countries. First, the official rates of interest in the organized sector of their credit markets should be raised high enough to reflect their existing shortage of capital funds. This would encourage the growth of a financial centre which can effectively attract savings both from within the country and from abroad. It would also serve to equate the available supply of savings to the demand for loans including the demand for funds by the money-lenders to be re-lent to the unorganized credit market. Second, a more integrated domestic market can be created only by giving free access on equal terms to the available funds both to the modern and the traditional sectors. The interest rates in the traditional sector can be more effectively reduced not by giving limited amounts of low-interest loans to the cooperative societies but by giving unlimited access on equal terms both to the cooperatives and the money-lenders so that they can compete to lower the interest rates for the small borrowers.

إلى هدى لنا

6

POPULATION PRESSURE AND AGGREGATE
CAPITAL REQUIREMENTS

The major driving force behind the study of the underdeveloped countries in the post-war years has been the desire to show that something should be done urgently to relieve their poverty. It is not difficult to understand, therefore, why the case of the overpopulated countries should come to be adopted as the prototype for all under-developed countries. With their acute material poverty, it is difficult at first sight to imagine how the overpopulated countries can increase their savings without grave hardships. On the other hand, their surplus population on the land seems to offer a major unused potential for economic development, waiting only for the 'missing component' of outside capital to assist them in the process. More-over, their rapid rates of population growth lend themselves to calculations of aggregate capital requirements which must be made available if their per capita incomes are to be maintained or raised to a level determined by humanitarian considerations. All in all, the drama of the poor countries struggling at the minimum subsistence level and the need for a massive dose of outside capital to break the interlocking vicious circles which hold them down to that level does not attain its full tragic grandeur unless viewed against the back-ground of overpopulation.

In this chapter I shall examine the two leading ideas which have dominated the writings on this subject, particularly in the early 1950s —the concept of 'disguised unemployment', and the general proposi-tion that all underdeveloped countries need to save and invest not less than 10% of their aggregate national income to achieve economic development.

'Disguised unemployment' and underemployment

The concept of 'disguised unemployment' is not so widely accepted as it used to be in the early 1950s. Yet it requires clarification and critical examination as it is one of those concepts which still keep turning up in various contexts in the writing on the underdeveloped countries. The main ideas behind the concept may be summarized as follows. In the overpopulated countries with extreme overcrowding on land, the marginal product of labour in agriculture falls to zero or at least to a very low level. A considerable amount of rural surplus labour can therefore be removed for productive use elsewhere, in the construction of capital goods such as roads and irrigation works and in the manufacturing sector. Where the marginal product of labour in the agricultural sector is zero, surplus labour can be removed without reducing the total agricultural output. But even if the marginal product of the surplus labour in agriculture is positive, it consumes more than it produces in subsistence agriculture, i.e. its consumption, equal to its average product, is much higher than its marginal product. Thus the removal of surplus labour will leave more food for those remaining on the land. In any case, therefore, a food surplus can be extracted without reducing the per capita consumption in subsistence agriculture, and this food surplus can then be used to feed the labour removed for productive work. 'Disguised unemployment' therefore provides 'concealed savings' which can be used to promote economic development in a 'costless' way, and this without any fundamental improvements in agricultural techniques.

At the outset, one thing should be made clear. A very considerable part of what is regarded as 'disguised unemployment' in agriculture is seasonal unemployment. Now the amount of seasonal unemployment depends not simply on the population density on land, but on other factors such as climate and rainfall, the availability of irrigation water and the general level of agricultural techniques determining the number of crops which can be grown on the same piece of land during the year. Thus, irrespective of population pressure on land, there would be a large amount of seasonal unemployment in countries which grow only a single crop a year. On the other hand, very densely populated countries such as Taiwan have been able to reduce seasonal unemployment on land drastically by growing a series of different crops on the same piece of land, based on better irrigation, the use of quick maturing seeds and the application of fertilizer. This serves to remind us that population pressure on land cannot really be satisfactorily defined without referring to agricultural techniques which determine the degree of labour intensity and multiple cropping on the same land.

Turning now to the conventional setting of the densely populated countries the chief conceptual weakness of 'disguised unemployment' arises from a failure to distinguish clearly between the zero marginal product of a unit of labour and the zero marginal product of a worker. This can be seen by taking a simple arithmetical example. Suppose that when 30 hours of work is put into a family holding, the marginal product of the 30th hour falls to zero. Assume that there are 6 workers in the family, sharing the work and output equally, so that each has to work 5 hours a day. Now with given agricultural techniques, the total output of the farm will remain unchanged as successive workers are removed, provided that the remaining workers work harder and longer to make up the total of 30 hours a day.

The first point which emerges is that there is nothing wrong with applying labour to land until the marginal product of the 30th hour of work falls to zero. Since no wages are paid and labour is free within the family, it will in fact be wasteful not to squeeze the most out of the scarce factor, land, until the marginal product of the abundant factor, labour, falls to zero. The possible waste in this situation arises not because the marginal product of the 30th hour of labour falls to zero, but because by working only 5 hours of the day, each of the 6 members of the family may be underemployed. The amount of 'disguised unemployment' depends on what we consider to be a full day's work for each. If we consider this to be 6 hours a day, there is disguised unemployment of one worker; if $7\frac{1}{2}$ hours a day, there is disguised unemployment of 2 workers; and if 10 hours a day, there is disguised unemployment of 3 workers.

Now the assumption that agricultural techniques remain unchanged merely means that the total output of the farm will remain unchanged so long as the total of 30 hours' work a day is performed. But in order to make those who remain on the land work harder to make up this total, there will have to be a considerable amount of reorganization, and provision of economic incentives. It should be noted that the number of hours which should be regarded as a 'full day's work' for those who remain behind is not unalterable. Depending on how efficiently the work is reorganized and how much economic incentives are offered, they may be induced to work 10 hours a day, making it possible to release 3 workers without reduction in total output; or $7\frac{1}{2}$ hours a day, releasing 2 workers; and so on. In the extreme case, where those who remain behind can obtain their minimum subsistence living by working only 5 hours each as before, and where no economic incentives are offered to induce them to work harder, it may not be possible to remove 'disguised unemployment' without some reduction in agricultural output.

This creates serious difficulties for the argument that the social cost of using disguised unemployment is zero. If we rely on positive economic incentives to induce those who remain on the land to work harder, then they would have to be provided with manufactured consumers' goods in exchange for their food surplus. The extra resources required for the production of these incentive consumers' goods constitute the social cost of keeping the agricultural output unchanged after the removal of disguised unemployment. If the proposal is to tax away the food surplus so that those who remain behind on the land cannot increase their per capita consumption, these forcible methods may work in the short run; but in the long run, there is likely to be a decline in agricultural output. It is very important to stress at this point that the problem of economic development cannot be solved simply by a once-for-all transfer of food surplus from the peasants to the government in a given year. A continuous and sustained process is required, in which the *growing* food surplus from the agricultural sector is made available to feed a growing number of non-agricultural workers. This is more likely to be achieved by encouraging the peasants into the money economy by positive incentives rather than forcible measures which may drive them further back into the subsistence economy. Moreover, economic incentives should be regarded not merely as the method of inducing the peasants to sell the food surplus obtained with their existing agricultural techniques, but more importantly as a method of inducing them to adopt better methods of production which will raise the food surplus in future.

Again, we may question the 'costless' nature of using 'disguised unemployment' when we turn to those who are removed from the land. It is now increasingly recognized that creating employment for them would not only require additional investment in the form of housing and equipment but would also generate extra consumption out of the new expanding wage incomes, adding to the total consumption of the community.[1] In a country like India, the social cost

[1] A. K. Sen, *Choice of Techniques*, 3rd ed., Oxford 1968, ch. 5.

created by this extra consumption is very concretely felt in the form of serious pressures on limited food supplies. Thus even if the use of 'disguised unemployment' did not reduce the total food supply, it would add to the total demand for food. And the creation of employment to absorb 'disguised unemployment' can be justified only if its extra output in the new occupations is large enough to cover the extra consumption which is generated. But the capital projects such as irrigation works and roads in which 'disguised unemployment' is to be used do not yield an immediately consumable output. We are then led to the problems of the social cost of waiting in relation to the size of the future income which will be considered in Chapter 8.

In addition to being regarded as the source of concealed saving for the construction of social overhead capital projects, 'disguised unemployment' is also regarded as the source of 'unlimited supplies of labour' for the manufacturing sector. Thus a well-known model of economic development put forward by Professor W. A. Lewis[1] starts from the presumption that the capital-intensive modern technology in the modern manufacturing industry will raise the productivity of labour above its low level in the traditional agricultural and handicraft sector. Since however 'unlimited supplies of labour' can be drawn from the traditional agricultural sector at a constant wage rate, this would enable the modern manufacturing sector to earn high profits: the reinvestment of these profits, drawing in further supplies of labour from the pool of disguised unemployment, is depicted as the mainspring of economic development. Here 'disguised unemployment' contributes to the increase in saving and investment indirectly, by providing 'unlimited supplies of labour' at a constant wage rate to the manufacturing sector enabling it to continue to earn high profits for further reinvestment. In the Lewis model the food supply required for the expanding labour force in the manufacturing sector is obtained by exchanging the manufactured consumers' goods for agricultural products and it is recognized that a 'balanced growth' between the output of the manufacturing and the agricultural sectors is crucial for sustaining the process of economic development.

Leaving the theory of 'balanced growth' to the later sections, it is necessary to make two points at this stage on the relation between

[1] W. A. Lewis, 'Economic development with unlimited supplies of labour', *The Manchester School*, May 1954.

'disguised unemployment' and the expansion of the manufacturing sector.

First, the emphasis on 'disguised unemployment' and the availability of 'unlimited supplies' of labour at a constant wage to the manufacturing sector distracts attention from the important point that labour supply can play merely a passive role in the process of industrial expansion. The real mainspring of this process is to be found in the ability of the manufacturing sector to raise labour productivity and earn high profits. The crucial question is how far the adoption of modern capital-intensive technology by itself would raise labour productivity in the manufacturing sector and enable it to earn high profits for reinvestment. Thus, we get back to the fundamental problem of the underdeveloped countries' capacity to absorb capital and modern technology. Where this absorptive capacity is lacking and where the inefficient and non-competitive manufacturing industries can be kept alive only by heavy protection, subsidies and import restrictions, the existence of the 'disguised unemployment' is not a sufficient condition for a sustained expansion of the manufacturing sector.

Second, as we have seen in the last chapter, in their attempt to promote domestic industrialization, many underdeveloped countries have followed the policies which aggravate the economic dualism between the modern manufacturing sector characterized by low interest rates and high wages and the traditional agricultural sector characterized by high interest rates and low wages. This dualism introduces a dangerous twist into the process of the transfer of labour from the agricultural to the manufacturing sector.

The Lewis model assumes that the gap between the wage level in the manufacturing sector and the per capita income level in the traditional agricultural sector is just sufficient to cover the higher cost of living in towns and provide the minimum inducement necessary to attract labour from the agricultural sector. In practice, however, in most underdeveloped countries wages in the manufacturing sector are, on the average, about twice as high as the income levels in the agricultural sector and are generally well in excess of the minimum differential in incomes required to attract labour from agriculture to manufacture. This has been brought about by various factors. Trade unions are stronger in the urban manufacturing industries and governments frequently pass minimum wage laws which can be strictly enforced in the larger corporations in the modern sector. The upward pressure of wages in the prosperous mining and petroleum export industries where they exist is transmitted to the modern manufacturing sector through a 'sympathetic' rise in wages. Frequently the large foreign-owned manufacturing corporations are prepared to pay a high wage differential to retain their existing labour force which has already acquired experience, skills and discipline. They also find it uneconomic to redesign their entire production and organizational framework based on the capital-intensive technology originating in the high wage conditions of the advanced countries to suit the local conditions of the underdeveloped countries.

Whatever the reason, the excessive wage differential in the manufacturing sector attracts a growing stream of labour from the agricultural sector, reinforced by the spread of education and literacy to the rural areas and the attraction of the amenities of life in the cities. Given the highly capital-intensive or labour-saving nature of the technology which prevails in the modern manufacturing sector, the expansion of that sector can provide employment only to a small fraction of the growing stream of job seekers. Thus, most underdeveloped countries are now experiencing the process by which the migration of labour from agriculture to manufacturing industry has converted the 'disguised unemployment' of the rural areas into the open unemployment in the shanty towns around the big cities. Nor has the failure to get well-paid jobs in the cities appreciably slowed down the inflow of immigrants from the rural areas, since many prefer to wait and try their luck at the somewhat slender prospect of getting a well-paid job rather than to return to their villages. Now while the 'disguised unemployeds' in the rural areas are supported by their relatives and the informal social welfare system of the subsistence sector, the jobless in the urban centres are in a worse plight. The growing pool of urban unemployment becomes a natural source of social and political tensions and resentment even in the underdeveloped countries which are expanding rapidly in terms of aggregate national product and per capita incomes.

The simple answer that the manufacturing sector should be expanded at a faster rate to absorb increasing unemployment is not likely to be effective. So long as the excessively wide wage differential exists between the modern manufacturing sector and the traditional agricultural sector, the migration of labour into the former from the latter would continue and the expansion of the manufacturing sector at the existing wage differentials would merely attract new entrants to swell the pool of urban unemployment to replace those

who gained employment. The only satisfactory method of reducing
the inflow of rural labour is to narrow the wage differential. This
can be done by removing or controlling the artificial factors which
have contributed to the high wages in the manufacturing sector,
notably the minimum wage laws and trade union pressure and partly
by policies to raise the level of earnings and productivity in the
agricultural sector.

This leads us to the second way in which the doctrine 'disguised
unemployment' has distracted attention from a more important
problem of economic development, viz. the raising of productivity in
the agricultural sector. Lured by the hope of getting something for
nothing, the exponents of the 'disguised unemployment' theory have
concentrated on how to extract the labour surplus and the food
surplus from the agricultural sector and have made a great point of
saying that this can be done without any improvement in agricultural techniques. In contrast we shall see that the introduction of
more efficient techniques raising the productivity of the agricultural
sector is the key to the successful process of the transfer of labour
from agriculture to manufacture.

Aggregate capital requirements and the capital–output ratio
With the idea of capital as the 'missing component' of economic
development which prevailed in the earlier post-war period, it was
natural that economists should try to make estimates of the aggregate capital requirements of the developing countries, globally[1] and
for each individual country. The most influential formula for an
individual developing country was that it should save and invest not
less than 10% to 12% of its national income. This was one of the
three conditions for the 'take-off' laid down by Professor W. W.
Rostow, and Professor W. A. Lewis put forward his well-known
dictum that 'the central problem in the theory of economic growth is
to understand the process by which a community is converted from
being a 5% to a 12% saver—with all the changes in attitudes, in
institutions and in techniques which accompany this conversion'.[2]

What was not clearly explained was that this formula can be
arrived at in two significantly different ways. Professor Rostow's

[1] For the earliest and most well-known example of global calculations see
United Nations Report on *Measures for Economic Development of Underdeveloped Countries*, 1951, ch. 11, Table 2.
[2] W. A. Lewis, *Theory of Economic Growth*, London 1959, pp. 225–6.

argument is based mainly on the historical analogy with the advanced countries in their take-off phase in the past, during which they had not only saved and invested more than 10% of their national income but, what is more important, *held on* to this high rate of savings and investment for two or three decades.   It is a part of the intense economic effort which a developing country should make to launch itself into the take-off process which involves sharp and *discontinuous* changes in the production structure. On the other hand, the formula may also be arrived at by using the *stable* overall capital–output ratio on the Harrod–Domar growth model designed for the later 'mature' phase of the advanced countries after they have taken-off into steady growth. If the population of an underdeveloped country is growing at 2% per annum, its total national income must also be growing at 2% per annum to maintain its per capita income at the same level. If it is further desired that on humanitarian or political grounds, the per capita income itself should be raised by 2% per annum, then the total national income of the country should be growing approximately at 4% per annum. Now assume that in order to obtain an extra £1 worth of income the country requires to make an investment of £3, averaging out the different capital requirements between the different sectors of the economy—that is to say, its overall incremental capital–output ratio is 3. In order to raise the per capita income at the target rate of 2% per annum, requiring a 4% rate of increase in total income to take into account population increase, the country should be saving and investing $3 \times 4\% = 12\%$ of its national income each year.

Many writers have urged the developing countries to save and invest not less than 10% to 12% of the national income without explaining whether they are giving this advice (1) on the basis of the take-off theory implying sharp discontinuous changes in the production structure, or (2) on the basis of a stable capital–output ratio implying a process of continuous steady economic growth. They shift freely between these two approaches, ignoring the fact that the 'take-off' phase (1) is separated by many decades of development from the 'mature' phase (2). Nor have they been troubled by the fact that neither (1) nor (2) might be applicable to many of the underdeveloped countries which are still at the earlier 'pre-take-off' stage.

(1) After our analysis of the earlier stages of the development of the money and the wage economy, we should now have a clearer appreciation of the fact that the underdeveloped countries are at very

different stages of general economic development. A few of the relatively more advanced among them, such as Taiwan, South Korea, Mexico or Brazil, may be somewhere within striking distance of the 'take-off' phase. But many more of them are still in the various stages of building their runway for the take-off. In particular, they lack the basic political, 'social and institutional framework' which both Professor Rostow and Professor Lewis would regard as the essential preconditions of the take-off. For instance, some of the underdeveloped countries are not yet able to maintain efficient law and order, whereas Professor Cairncross has reminded us, 'most countries that have staged a successful take-off have enjoyed an antecedent period of domestic peace which prevented the periodical destruction of physical assets and gave security to investment'.[1] Further, one of the less clearly appreciated aspects of Professor Rostow's theory is that, according to the historical examples he has given, a successful take-off requires not merely raising the saving and investment ratio above 10% of national income but maintaining it at that level for two or three decades. This requires a much higher ability not only to mobilize saving but also to invest it more effectively than the underdeveloped countries with their weak administrative, fiscal and monetary framework can be expected to have.

This, of course, does not mean that because countries are at the earlier stages of general development, they should not try to increase their rate of saving and investment. There are obvious fields: improvements in transport and communications alone can absorb a great deal of capital, both foreign and domestic. Again there are the 'pre-investments' in health, education, training and research, designed to increase 'human capital' and improve the country's capacity to absorb further investment. But nevertheless it is important to recognize that a country's progress towards economic development cannot be judged simply by an overall ratio of saving and investment to national income without taking into account the qualitative and less easily measurable factors such as the efficiency and honesty of its administration, the degree of its political and monetary stability, or the skills and attitudes of the people. Nor is it wise to apply a mechanical rule-of-thumb which only represents one aspect of the take-off theory to all the underdeveloped countries at different stages of the pre-take-off period.

(2) One obvious objection which can be made to the method of calculating the aggregate capital requirements of the underdeveloped

[1] A. K. Cairncross, *Factors in Economic Development*, London 1962, p. 120.

countries on the basis of a stable overall capital–output ratio is that this implies the assumption of constant returns to scale for the expansion of the economy as a whole. This assumption is justified for the mature phase of the advanced countries to which the Harrod–Domar growth model is intended to apply. For these countries, primary production, which is subject to diminishing returns, forms a small part of their total output. Besides, technical progress and economies of scale are 'built in' to their economic life so that we can expect the forces for increasing returns to counteract the forces for diminishing returns. This is in fact confirmed by the advanced countries' experience of a steady and self-sustained process of economic growth for many decades. In contrast, one of the most well-established propositions about the underdeveloped countries is that agriculture and primary production forms the larger part of their national outputs and that *given unchanged techniques* the pressure of population increase on their given natural resources will result in conditions of diminishing returns to scale for the expansion of the economy as a whole.

This is as old as the Ricardian theory of the stationary state. It will be remembered that in the Ricardian theory, investment is looked upon not as the addition to the durable capital equipment, but mainly as the addition to the wage-fund or the subsistence-fund to be used to maintain a larger number of workers. The rate of profit on investment is measured by the difference between the marginal product of labour in agriculture and its wage rate (both measured in terms of the 'corn' or the general subsistence fund). As investment increases and more workers are put to work on the land, with given techniques the marginal product of labour will fall until it is equal to its wages. At this point, the rate of profit on investment falls to zero. This tendency to a declining rate of profit in agriculture is transmitted to the rest of the economy, particularly to the manufacturing sector, in the following way. Because of diminishing returns the rate of expansion in the agricultural output tends to lag behind that of the manufactured goods. This will raise the price of foodstuffs and raw materials in relation to the price of manufactured goods, and so raise the cost of living for the workers employed in the manufacturing sector. In order to maintain the same real wage level, therefore, their money wages will have to be raised proportionately to the rise in price of subsistence goods and this will lead to a decline in the rate of profit on investment in the manufacturing sector. Once the general rate of profits has fallen to zero, there will be no further incentive to increase investment and the economy approaches the stationary equilibrium.

In the language of the balanced growth theory (see Chapter 8) the Ricardian stationary state is brought about by the failure to expand the agricultural sector in a 'balanced growth' relation with the manufacturing sector, turning the intersectoral 'terms of trade' against the manufacturing sector. In the language of the capital–output ratio approach this means that diminishing returns which raise the cost of food for labour which enters into the production of the intermediate goods and capital goods will result in an increasing overall capital–output ratio as the economy expands. That is to say, we cannot apply the assumption of a stable overall capital–output ratio to the underdeveloped countries unless we can show at the same time how to counteract the general tendency towards diminishing returns. This becomes even more important when we remember that in many of these countries diminishing returns is not merely a matter of an increasing population pressing on a *given* amount of natural resources; the total available amount of natural resources is itself progressively reduced over time, because of overutilization and depletion through soil erosion, deforestation, or lowering of water tables, for example, not to mention the normal using up process of the mineral resources. In the language of the growth models, the assumption of a stable overall capital–output ratio for the under-developed countries requires not only that a continual stream of innovations is taking place, but that they are of a land-saving charac-ter, enabling a progressive substitution of capital and labour for natural resources.

In spite of this objection, the concept of an overall capital–output ratio has enjoyed a considerable vogue and it is frequently defended on the ground that it offers a useful basis for testing the consistency of the desired target rate of growth in national income and the available resources of a developing country. But in practice, we cannot get very far in testing the economic development plans of a country unless we are prepared to go behind the overall ratio into the structural factors which determine it.

The national income or output is not a homogeneous thing but is made up of different goods and services, each having widely varying capital–output ratios. The sectoral capital–output ratios are very high for some items, notably transport and communications and public utilities. Next in order of high capital–output ratios come housing and capital-goods industries. Manufactured consumers' goods industries together with other distributive and service industries generally have lower capital–output ratios.[1] The capital–output ratio in the agricultural sector of the underdeveloped countries is generally likely to be low, although some of the big irrigation and river valley projects require vast sums of capital. Characteristically, the expansion of agricultural output in these countries depends not only on capital inputs such as fertilizers and improved equipment, but also on improvements in technical knowledge, marketing, credit, or land tenure, for example, which are not directly reflected in the capital–output ratio.

Now the overall capital–output ratio is nothing but the average of these different sectoral capital–output ratios weighted according to the quantities of the different goods and services which are to be produced. Thus, before we can calculate the overall ratio we must specify the proportions of the different constituent items which are to make up a proposed rate of increase in the national output. But this barely scratches the surface of the problem of testing the consistency of an integrated economic development plan. For one thing, the target figures of increase in outputs of various items are not given independently of each other. Many of them are required not only for final consumption but also as intermediate goods or inputs in the production of other items. In testing, therefore, the consistency of the target figures of items and the resources available for them, we must take into account not only the direct requirements but also the

[1] W. B. Reddaway gives the following sectoral capital–output ratios for the third Indian five-year plan which has adopted an overall capital–output ratio of 2·2: Agriculture, 0·9; Mining and Manufacturing, 2·6; Small industries and Construction, 1·0; Railways and Communications, 6·5; Housing, 18·0; Other services, including Schools, Hospitals and Roads, 2·0. *The Development of the Indian Economy*, London 1962, p. 211. It may be noted that Housing, Railways and Communications have a very high capital–output ratio. In other countries, electricity generation and supply tends to have a very high capital–output ratio (cf. S. A. Abbas, *Capital Requirements for the Development of South and South-East Asia*, Groningen 1955, pp. 140–4). It may also be noted that, in general, manufacturing and mining industries require a relatively modest share of total investment, about a quarter of it, while the share of housing can be quite as much (cf. Colin Clark, *Conditions of Economic Progress*, 3rd ed., London 1940, pp. 604–5). The difficulties of calculating the sectoral capital–output ratios arise not only from paucity of statistical information but also from conceptual difficulties. Thus the high capital–output ratios in transport and communications should be counterbalanced by the economizing of capital stocks and inventories in other sectors, notably in commerce and distributive industries. Then there are doubtful borderline cases like fertilizer production which can be put either in the agricultural sector or in chemical industries.

indirect requirements of capital. Further, these complex input–output relationships should be tested not only for a given year, but continuously over the whole period of the plan. This means that for each of the intervening years, say, during a five-year plan, the rates of expansion of the different sectors must be phased so that they dovetail into each other, without any sector lagging behind their concerted timetable and holding up the others. For if this happens, shortages and excess capacities will develop and this will alter the effective capital–output ratios in the sectors which have gone out of alignment with the general plan. By the time we have gone through the consistency of an integrated development plan in this way, it does not help us much further to 'sum up the whole thing' in the form of an overall capital–output ratio.[1]

Yet a great deal of importance has been attached to this ratio, and the real reason seems to be that it offers a convenient shorthand basis for making out the case for increasing economic aid to the underdeveloped countries. But the concept of a stable overall capital–output ratio belongs to steady-growth models. As Professor Kuznets has recently shown, in terms of the conventional growth arithmetic, the extra savings a country would require to cater for an increase in population growth or to raise the growth rate in per capita income turns out to be surprisingly small. For his illustrative calculations, Kuznets adopts the commonly accepted capital–output ratio of 3. He takes a country with a 2% growth rate in per capita income and asks how much extra savings such a country would require to maintain its given rate of growth in income, if its population growth is increased from 1% to 3%. By making appropriate allowances for the change in population structure, he estimates that even with such a big increase in population growth, this country would need to reduce its consumption only by about 16%. This means 'the sacrifice of half of the long-term increase of 2% in per unit consumption for a decade and a half'. Kuznets next considers a country with 0·1% rate of growth in per capita income and a 3% population growth and asks how much extra savings such a country would require to raise the growth of its per capita income from 0·1% to 2%. He estimates that this would only require a reduction in per unit consumption of 7% (measured in terms of adult consumption units) which could be made up in about three years. Indeed, Kuznets is so struck by the smallness of the extra savings required in both cases that he asks why, if it is a realistic model of economic growth, so few countries have become developed, since 'the sacrifice of a small

[1] Reddaway, op. cit., Appendix C, for a further discussion of this concept.

fraction of rapidly growing consumption would hardly tax the energies or the social capacity of the least developed countries and societies'. Kuznets concludes that the steady growth models based on constant capital-output ratios are extremely unrealistic and that the reason why so few countries have become developed must be found, not in their lack of capacity to increase savings but in their inadequate institutional framework and their inability to provide the minimum of political stability and efficiency required for sustained growth.[1]

Since the early 1950s, many economists have been moving away from their simpler views of the 'capital shortage' of the underdeveloped countries based on calculations of aggregate capital requirements and overall capital–output ratios. There are many reasons for this.

First, there is now a greater recognition of the fact that a developing country's ability to save does not depend only on the level of its average national income but also on other factors such as the pattern of income distribution, the ability of the government to mobilize savings through taxation and the ability of the financial institutions making up the capital market to mobilize private savings. Second, as a matter of historical fact, the underdeveloped countries have been increasing their savings more rapidly than it was thought possible in the early 1950s and their average rate of savings rose to 15% of their GNP during the period 1960–7. Thus the target saving rate of 10% to 12% of the GNP has been achieved or surpassed by many countries and the notion of capital as the 'missing component' of economic development has become increasingly questionable. However, since the first meeting of the United Nations Conference on Trade and Development (UNCTAD), a new 'missing component' has been popularized. It is now argued that the economic development of the underdeveloped countries has been held back not so much by shortage of savings in general as by a shortage of particular types of capital goods, such as machinery and technically necessary inputs for their domestic manufacturing industry which they need to import from abroad. Thus 'foreign exchange shortage' has become the new and distinct missing component instead of the savings shortage.

[1] S. Kuznets, 'Population and Economic Growth', reprinted as Chapter 1 of his *Population, Capital and Growth*, London 1974; see particularly pp. 10–17 and pp. 34–6.

As we have seen in Chapter 5, normally one would attribute the balance-of-payments difficulties of the underdeveloped countries to their domestic inflation caused by government budget deficit, reinforced by the over-valuation of their currencies at the fixed official exchange rate. This implies that there is no real basis for distinguishing a 'foreign exchange shortage' from a 'savings shortage'. Both are the result of an excess of aggregate domestic demand over the available resources: the 'foreign exchange shortage' is merely the excess domestic demand for imports. Both can be remedied by appropriate fiscal and monetary policies to be adopted by the underdeveloped countries themselves.

But this standard analysis is unacceptable to the exponents of the 'foreign exchange shortage' theory who are concerned to show that the underdeveloped countries suffer from a foreign exchange 'gap' owing to external world market factors and technological imperatives of economic development beyond the control of their domestic economic policies. Their argument is based on two assumptions: (1) that the world market demand for primary exports from the underdeveloped countries is so inelastic that there is no possibility of increasing their foreign exchange earnings by increasing efficiency in export production and lowering the prices of the exports; (2) that there is a fixed relationship between the capital goods and inputs which have to be imported and the size of the domestic output, determined purely by technological factors. Thus a given target rate of growth in total output requires an irreducible minimum rate of growth in foreign exchange requirements. Since the expansion in exports is insufficient to supply this minimum rate of growth in foreign exchange requirements, the 'gap' can be filled only by more liberal international trade and aid policies by the advanced countries.

(1) As we shall see in Chapter 9, the 'export pessimism' which underlies the 'foreign exchange shortage' theory is unjustifiable for various reasons. For the moment, we may merely note that, during the 1960s, the export earnings of the underdeveloped countries were increasing at 6% per annum, a rate 50% higher than the original UNCTAD projections.

(2) A serious question is begged by the assumption of the given and fixed technical coefficients which underlies both the concept of the capital–output ratio and the concept of the irreducible minimum of imports required to achieve a target rate of growth in output. If the aim of economic planning is to make a more efficient use of the

available resources, it is not sufficient merely to test the consistency of the economic plan by accepting the given ratios of capital and foreign exchange requirements and the given target rates of growth in the different items of output. First, it would be necessary to inquire whether these ratios of capital and foreign exchange requirements to output can be regarded as the most economical way of using capital and foreign exchange in combination with the other factors of production. Here, as we have seen in Chapter 5, most underdeveloped countries have tried to promote domestic industrialization by providing capital and foreign exchange on excessively favourable terms to the manufacturing sector and this has encouraged the adoption of excessively capital-intensive methods of production requiring a correspondingly excessive amount of imported capital goods and other inputs. Secondly, except in a closed economy without any international trade, it is not sufficient to accept the target rates of growth in various items of output without asking whether some of these items may not be more cheaply acquired through international trade instead of domestic production. Thus the relevant economic question is not how much capital and foreign exchange would be required to run the existing manufacturing industries at their full technical capacity or to continue with a given rate of import substitution but whether the capital and the foreign exchange devoted to these industries or to the continuation of the import substitution policies represent the most efficient way of using the resources of an underdeveloped country. These questions will be further considered in Chapter 9 on international trade.

7

THE CRITICAL MINIMUM EFFORT FOR
ECONOMIC DEVELOPMENT AND THE SIZE OF
THE BALANCED-GROWTH PROGRAMME

So far I have been concerned with the case for a large-scale development effort which is based either on the historical analogy with the
developed countries during their 'take-off' period, or on a desired
target rate of growth in per capita income determined by political
and humanitarian considerations. I shall now consider further
arguments for 'crash' economic development programmes based on
the general thesis that the underdeveloped countries are held down
very firmly to their low levels of per capita incomes by 'interlocking
vicious circles'. It is maintained that these vicious circles would
defeat any piecemeal attempt to promote economic development;
and that only a massive injection of capital on an all-or-nothing
basis to finance a development programme pushing simultaneously
ahead on a wide front could hope to break these vicious circles.

As we have seen in Chapter 1, the simple 'vicious circle' theory has
not been borne out by the economic experiences of the underdeveloped countries during 1950–75. Despite a rapid rate of population growth, they have as a group enjoyed an average growth rate
in per capita income of 3% per annum, although there are marked
variations in growth between different countries. Furthermore, there
is no simple association between the low level of per capita income
and low rate of economic growth as suggested by the vicious circle
of poverty approach. While some of the richer Latin American
countries have suffered a low rate of growth, some of the poorer
Asian countries such as Taiwan and Thailand have been enjoying
higher than average rates of growth. However, it is still useful to
consider two examples of the all-or-nothing approach based on the
vicious circle theory.

The first is concerned with the overall relation between the rate of growth in per capita income and the rate of growth in population, and emphasizes that while a small increase in per capita income would be swallowed up by the population increase induced by it, a large increase in per capita income created by a development programme exceeding a certain 'critical minimum effort' would escape the gravitational pull of population increase. The theory is perhaps more significant as an argument for the need to control population growth rather than as an argument for the need for a 'critical minimum effort' for economic development. The second goes behind the overall relations to the different aspects of the vicious circle, particularly the low purchasing power and smallness of the domestic market in the underdeveloped countries, and the indivisibilities and interdependence of capital investment required for economic development. Thus in order to overcome the limitations of the smallness of the domestic market created by low per capita incomes and to enjoy the internal economies of scale and the external economies of complementary investment, it is necessary to start with a large-scale development programme, simultaneously trying to push forward over a wide range of economic activities. This approach, based on the theory of 'balanced growth', underlies much of the thinking on development planning in the underdeveloped countries and requires to be carefully examined.

The low-level equilibrium trap and the critical minimum effort thesis[1]
Essentially, this theory is based on two propositions. (1) The first proposition starts from the Malthusian theorem that population will increase when the per capita income of a country rises above the 'minimum subsistence level'. But it then goes on to state that while initially population grows rapidly with a rise in per capita income, there is an upper physical limit to the rate of population growth, say at about 3% per annum. Beyond this limit a rise in per capita income will not be accompanied by a further rise in the rate of growth of population. On the contrary, the rate of population growth may even decline gradually with further rises in per capita income; this is suggested by the experience of the Western countries, and more recently by Japan.

(2) The second proposition consists of the familiar argument that at low levels of per capita income people are too poor to save and

[1] R. R. Nelson, 'A theory of the low level equilibrium trap', *American Economic Review*, December 1956; and H. Leibenstein, *A Theory of Economic–Demographic Development*, London 1954, and *Economic Backwardness and Economic Growth*, New York 1957.

invest much, and this low rate of investment will result in a low rate of growth in total national income. But as the per capita income rises above a certain minimum level at which there is zero saving a rising proportion of the total income will be saved and invested and this will lead to a higher rate of growth in income.

The argument may be illustrated by a set of diagrams. In diagram (a) the level of per capita income is measured on the horizontal axis and the percentage rate of growth of population on the vertical axis. The point S on the horizontal axis denotes the minimum subsistence level of per capita income. Below this level of income to the left of S, population will be decreasing, and at S population will be stationary. But as we move to the right of S, denoting a rise in the per capita income above the subsistence level, the rate of population growth depicted by the PP′ curve will increase until it reaches the upper physical limit around 3% after which it may decline gradually. In diagram (b) the level of per capita income is measured on the horizontal axis as before, but the vertical axis measures the per capita rate of investment out of savings at different levels of per capita income. The point X on the horizontal axis denotes the level of income with zero saving. Until this level of income is reached, all income will be spent on consumption, and below this level, to the left of X, there is negative investment, or living on past capital. But as we move to the right of X, denoting a rise in the per capita income above the zero saving level, the per capita rate of investment, the II′ curve, will rise and there is no upper limit to it. As we move to the right of X, a rising proportion of the total income can be saved and invested, particularly beyond the point at which the rate of growth in population levels off at 3%. It is only at a later stage at a much higher income level that the proportion of total income saved and invested will settle down to a constant fraction.

There is no necessity for the minimum subsistence level of per capita income S to be the same as the zero saving level of per capita income X. But for simplicity's sake, I have drawn the diagram (c) on the assumption that the two coincide. Here, as before, the horizontal axis measures the level of per capita income. But on the vertical axis we are now measuring the percentage rate of growth in population and the percentage rate of growth in total income at the different levels of per capita income shown along the horizontal axis. As I have drawn the diagram, the point S (equal to X) on the horizontal axis represents the 'low-level equilibrium' trap. It denotes the intersection of the population growth curve PP′ and the income growth curve YY′ at the zero rate of growth. Starting from this,

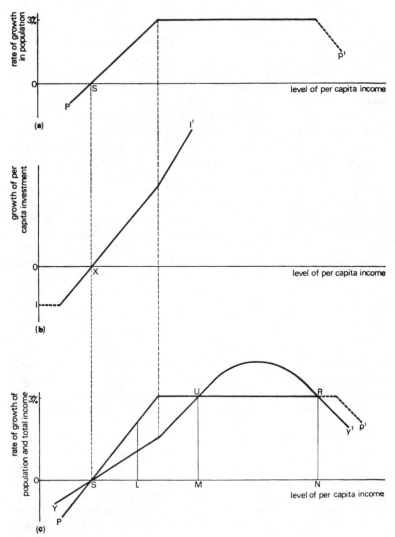

PP¹ = growth curve of population
II¹ = growth curve of investment
YY¹ = growth curve of total income

for any small rise in the level of per capita income, say of SL, the rate of growth in population will be higher than the rate of growth in total income, pushing back the per capita income to its previous stable equilibrium level of OS. This low-level equilibrium trap will be stronger the more quickly the rate of population growth responds to a given rise in per capita income and the more slowly the rate of growth in total income responds to an increase in investment, due, say, to initial population pressure on land. But if it were possible to raise the level of per capita income by a discontinuous jump by more than SM, which means pushing the rate of increase in income beyond the population barrier of 3%, then we should have arrived at a new unstable equilibrium at U. A rise in the level of per capita income beyond OM, being unaccompanied by a further rise in the rate of population growth, would then lead to a cumulative process of rising income until possibly it reached a new stable equilibrium point R with a per capita income level of ON.

The 'critical minimum effort' theory has given us a very neat formalization of the vicious circle of low per capita income, leading to low rates of saving and investment, leading to a low per capita income. But it raises two sets of difficulties.

First, we may question whether it is possible to draw a rigid functional relation between the level of per capita income and the rate of growth of population and the rate of growth in total income. As we have seen in Chapter 2, the main cause of growth in population has been the reduction in death rates due to improvements in public health and the control of epidemics and endemics, which are not closely related to a prior rise in per capita income level. The tendency of a rise in per capita income to *lower* birth rates at higher income levels needs to be interpreted even more cautiously. But we may on the whole accept the upper physical limit to the rate of population growth around 3% per annum, provided it is clearly understood that even beyond this point the absolute size of population would continue to grow at a constant or slowly diminishing rate, continuing to exert its pressure on the given natural resources. The functional relationship between the level of per capita income and the rate of growth in total income is more complex and takes place in two steps. The relation between the level of per capita income and the rate of saving and investment is modified by a number of factors such as the pattern of distribution of incomes and the effectiveness of financial institutions in mobilizing savings. The relation between investment and the resultant output is also not given by a stable overall capital–output ratio, but depends on how far the productive organization of the country can be improved and how far land-saving innovations can be adopted to overcome the tendency to diminishing returns on additional investment which will continue even after the population growth has levelled off at 3% per annum.

The second set of difficulties arises from the complications introduced by the 'time element'. It may be noted that the diagrams illustrate a set of 'timeless' functional relationships rather than the time-series of growth in population and income. Further, the analytical device of using two reaction curves which intersect first at a 'stable' and then at an 'unstable' equilibrium as in diagram (c) is borrowed from the trade cycle theory designed to deal with turning points in the level of short-run economic activity in the advanced countries—from a state of depression through an 'upswing' phase to a boom and so on.[1] We may therefore question how far this type of analysis, originally designed to illustrate the gear-shifts in short-run economic activity of a fully developed engine of growth in the advanced countries, is useful for the study of the problem of the long-term economic development of the underdeveloped countries which is concerned with the construction of the engine of growth itself.

Two specific points may be raised. Consider first a 'small' rise in the level of per capita income from S to an intermediate point L below OM in diagram (c). This will lead back to the 'stable' equilibrium point S only if we interpret the curves as timeless and reversible relations. If we take the time factor into account, the rise of income from S to L may be accompanied by permanent and 'irreversible' additions to the capital stock and skills. In this case, things will not be exactly the same as before and the economy may not revert to the previous level of per capita income S but may stay at a point above it. Once we admit the possibility of the 'ratchet effect',[2] the case for a large 'critical minimum effort' to reach OM at one go is considerably weakened since we may be able to get there by a series of smaller steps supported by a ratchet at each step. Next, consider that by a massive development programme a country has succeeded for a time in raising the rate of growth in its total income above the 3% per annum rate which represents the population barrier. Does this really mean that at the per capita level above OM it has now automatically entered a new 'unstable' phase of cumulative upward

[1] e.g., N. Kaldor, 'A model of the trade cycle', *Economic Journal*, March 1940.
[2] I owe this point to Mr A. D. Knox.

rise in income? Clearly this is not so since it is not difficult to find examples of abortive 'take-offs' in which a country may for a time succeed in raising its saving and investment ratio above 10% to 12% and raising the rate of growth in its total income above the 3% level, but subsequently relapse into a slower rate of growth and stagnation. How long must a country sustain its rate of growth above the 3% level before it can be sure of breaking through the population barrier? Whatever its drawbacks, the 'take-off' theory at least suggests by means of historical examples that this effort has to be sustained for two or three decades during which fundamental reorganizations in the institutional and productive structure should be taking place. On the other hand, the 'critical minimum effort' theory does not concern itself with these important qualitative problems of the changes in economic and social organization necessary for sustained economic development.

Finally, it is necessary to re-examine the implicit assumption of the 'critical minimum effort' theory that population growth, determined by autonomous social forces, would inevitably tend towards its maximum limit of 3% in the underdeveloped countries and that therefore all we can do to raise the level of per capita income is to concentrate exclusively on crash investment programmes to raise total output. But in recent times there have been significant technical advances in various methods of birth control and encouraging examples of underdeveloped countries which have been able to reduce their population growth by vigorous government policies. For instance, within one decade, Singapore has successfully brought down her population growth to 1·5% per annum. Thus it does not appear to be too unrealistic to ask whether the underdeveloped countries might not more effectively raise the rate of growth in their per capita income by investment designed to reduce population growth rather than by concentrating simply on investment to increase their total national product.[1]

In terms of the geometric model of the 'critical minimum effort' theory, a reduction in the rate of population growth would bring about two economic advantages: (1) it would reduce the critical minimum size of investment required to jerk the economy out of its

[1] For persuasive statements of this view, see S. Enke, 'The economic aspects of slowing population growth', *Economic Journal*, March 1966; G. Ohlin, *Population Control and Economic Development*, OECD, Paris 1966; and A. J. Coale and E. M. Hoover, *Population Growth and Economic Development in Low-Income Countries*, Princeton, New Jersey 1958.

initial low-income equilibrium trap and (2) it would enable the economy to enjoy a higher longer-run level of per capita income when it settled down to the new stable equilibrium position. This can be seen by referring to diagram (c). Assuming the same growth curve for total income YY', a downward shift in the population growth curve PP' below the 3% level will have the effect (1) of reducing the distance between the stable equilibrium point S and the unstable equilibrium point U, and (2) of making the income growth curve YY' intersect with the lower population growth curve (not drawn on the diagram) at a new stable equilibrium point representing a higher level of per capita income than ON.

The size of the balanced growth

Balanced-growth theory may refer to the minimum *size* of the investment programme required to start economic development. Or it may refer to the *path* of economic development and the pattern of investment necessary to keep the different sectors of the economy in a balanced growth relation with each other. I shall start with the first aspect of the theory which stresses the need for an all-or-nothing approach to economic development. It is possible to distinguish at least three related versions of the theory, each suggesting a progressively larger aggregate size of the balanced-growth investment programme than its predecessor.

(1) The earliest and the narrowest version of the theory is to be found in Professor P. N. Rosenstein-Rodan's well-known article first published in 1943.[1] The central idea here is the need to overcome the smallness in the size of the market created by the low per capita income and purchasing power of consumers in the underdeveloped countries. He argues that a single factory, even when it uses more efficient methods of production than the handicraft industry, may fail when set up on its own because of the smallness of the market outlet for its output. What is needed is the simultaneous setting up of a number of factories producing different consumers' goods so that between them they create enough new employment and purchasing power to provide a sufficiently large market for each other. This is the narrowest version of the theory in that it confines the balanced-growth programme to the production of light consumers' goods. It was assumed that Eastern and South-Eastern Europe as a

[1] P. N. Rosenstein-Rodan, 'Problems of industrialization of Eastern and South-Eastern Europe', *Economic Journal*, 1943.

region would be exporting agricultural products and importing machinery and equipment from abroad so that heavy industry and agriculture were explicitly excluded from the framework of the programme. It was also assumed that the region as a whole was adequately supplied with transport, communications and power for the setting up of consumers' goods industries so that there was no need for costly investment in social overhead capital to support the programme. Considering the abundant supply of 'disguised unemployment' from agriculture, all that was needed was a sufficient inflow of outside capital to finance a sufficiently large balanced-growth programme in consumers' goods with markets for them from the whole region. The argument was that starting from the low levels of income and consumption of the people of the region, it would not be difficult to predict the extra amounts of different consumers' goods which they would demand with a rise in their incomes. It was also pointed out that by concentrating on the production of consumers' goods the balanced-growth approach would provide a less painful alternative to the 'communist model' of industrialization with its emphasis on setting up heavy capital goods industries at the expense of consumers' goods.

To get at the logical basis of the argument, let us start from the initial situation where the consumers' goods to be included in the balanced-growth programme were either produced by the handicraft industries or were imported at a *certain set of relative prices*. Starting from this, it is possible to think of two extreme cases showing the relative importance of pure cost reduction and pure income expansion for the success of the new industries.

First, let us suppose the rise of an especially capable entrepreneur or an improvement in the techniques of production in one of the consumers' goods industries. In this case, it is clearly possible for a single new factory producing this particular product to establish itself successfully, in spite of the prevailing low incomes and purchasing power of its customers. The total size of the market may be limited; but if the new factory is efficient enough, it can attract a share of this total market sufficient to enable it to use its machinery and fixed equipment to full capacity and reduce the cost per unit of its output to a minimum. By lowering its price, the new factory is able to attract customers, not only from the handicraft industry which was producing a similar product, but also from all other consumers' goods whose prices have remained the same as before. Through sheer efficiency and ability to reduce cost, a single new factory can establish itself successfully, relying mainly on the 'substitution effect' working through the price elasticity of demand for its product. In displacing the demand for some of the existing products, the new factory will cause some unemployment elsewhere; but, provided it can create enough new employment to offset this, the total income and purchasing power will be increased since the resources employed in the new factory now have higher productivity. But this favourable 'income effect' is likely to be of secondary importance to the success of the new factory.

Next, at the other extreme, let us think of setting up a large group of new factories producing different consumers' goods whose individual productive efficiency is not superior to that of the existing producers of these goods. These new factories would then have to rely on their combined ability to expand employment and purchasing power to be able to sell their products at the same prices as before. It will be seen that by relying mainly on the 'income effect', and without the ability to reduce costs and so attract the extra demand from outside the group, the new factories as a group are not likely to create enough extra purchasing power to be able to dispose of their combined output. First, since the value of the total output of the new factories is made up of wages and profit, expenditure out of the new wage income alone could not create a sufficient extra demand. This gap in purchasing power has to be filled by assuming that all the profits are re-invested and turned into wage-income elsewhere, say in the capital goods industries whose workers now become the customers for the newly produced consumers' goods. Further, in so far as the balanced-growth programme embraces only part of the economy, there would be leakages of purchasing power to other sectors outside its framework; say in the form of extra demand for food from the agricultural sector, the extra demand for the products of the handicraft and other indigenous industries, and the extra demand for imports.

The situation depicted in this version (1) of the balanced-growth theory seems to lie between these two cases of pure cost reduction and pure income expansion, but with considerable leanings towards pure income expansion. It does not assume any special improvements in the methods of production or the rise of a superior entrepreneurial class, for these would dispense with the need for a balanced growth programme. On the other hand, it does assume that merely by taking over the existing technical 'know-how' of the advanced countries, the new factories would normally be able to reduce their costs below the handicraft industries, provided that each could obtain individual markets large enough to expand output to full capacity production, reducing its cost per unit to a minimum.

I now come to the crucial link in the argument. By insisting that a large number of factories should be set up at the same time, the theory concentrates on the enlargement of the total volume of purchasing power and the *total size* of the market. On the other hand, the ability of each factory to obtain the economies of the modern factory method of production depends on its share of the total market: that is, on the size of its *individual* market. The theory then assumes too readily that, provided the size of the total market can be increased, the share of the individual market accruing to each factory will follow a set pattern of expansion in consumers' expenditure, determined by the income elasticity of demand for each product. Thus provided that the total volume of employment and purchasing power is increased by a 'minimum' indivisible step, each factory will have a large enough market to reach full capacity production and the point of minimum cost per unit. There are three weaknesses in this argument.

First, the introduction of the existing technical 'know-how' of the advanced countries to the different conditions that exist in the under-developed countries need not always result in the superiority of the modern factory method of production over the existing indigenous methods. It largely depends on how well these modern techniques are adapted to local conditions; that is, on the skill and quality of the entrepreneurs who run new factories. Again, in any given condition, the 'normal' superiority of factory methods over handicraft methods will vary widely between different commodities: given a large group of new factories, the capacity of each individual factory to reduce its cost below existing producers will vary very widely. At one end of the scale there would be 'stronger' factories which could almost stand up on their own, and at the other end of the scale there would be 'weaker' factories whose costs, even at full capacity production, would be barely below those of the handicraft industries. These weaker factories are the 'marginal' factories whose inclusion into the programme would have to be carefully examined. Secondly, for the type of light consumers' goods with which the version (1) of the theory is concerned, the 'substitution effect' and price elasticities of demand are likely to play a much larger role than the theory allows. Finally, there is no reason to suppose that the pattern of expansion of consumers' expenditure on different goods, determined by their respective income elasticities of demand, would fit in neatly with the pattern of expansion in the supplies of these goods, representing full-capacity production or the technically indivisible quantum of expansion for each. These disproportions can only be corrected through changes in relative prices.

Once we recognize the importance of the 'substitution effect' working through the changes in relative costs and prices and price elasticities of demand, the all-or-none approach to economic development formulated entirely in terms of the 'income effect' and income elasticities of demand becomes illusory. The whole argument seems to be incomplete and indeterminate if it does not take into account changes in the relative costs and prices. The success of the balanced-growth programme of type (1) depends not merely on how many factories are being set up at the same time, but more importantly on the varying degrees of superior efficiency each factory has over the existing producers, and on each factory's ability to counter the potential leakage of purchasing power outside by reductions in costs and prices.

But can we not go on expanding the size of the balanced-growth programme by setting up more factories until the sheer size of the 'income effect' overcomes the weakness of the 'substitution effect' in favour of the programme? It is worth emphasizing that even on the assumptions (a) that an 'unlimited' supply of labour would be available from 'disguised unemployment' and (b) that a sufficient amount of external capital would be forthcoming to pay for the machinery and capital equipment to be used for the production of consumers' goods, a continued expansion in the size of the programme is likely to be subject to sharply increasing costs for at least three reasons. First, as we have seen, the increasing volume of employment in the new factories would be likely to increase the pressure of demand for food and, in so far as agriculture is subject to diminishing returns, this would raise the cost of living and the money wage costs in the manufacturing sector in the Ricardian manner. Secondly, even if a large number of factories were to create economies in the training and 'skilling' of labour in the longer run, the immediate effect would be for each factory to bid up the wages of the scarce skilled labour and create external diseconomies for each other. Finally, there is likely to be a serious shortage of suitable entreprenuers and managers for the factories, and as less able people were recruited to these positions there would be a general decline in efficiency and an increase in costs. Thus, the possible favourable income effect of increasing the size of the programme has to be weighed against the possible sharp rise in costs as an increasing number of factories compete for scarce resources in the form of food supply, skilled labour and entrepreneurs and managers. Instead of an all-or-none approach, we are led back to the more familiar procedure of making economic choices between a smaller and a larger size of development plan, even if this is a more rough-and-ready process than the traditional marginal calculus in terms of very small incremental gains and losses.

(2) As soon as the first version of the balanced-growth theory is applied to the underdeveloped countries of Asia and Africa with their inadequate transport and communication and power supply, its exponents feel the need to extend its framework to include investment in these 'social overhead' services. Now investment of this type is notoriously 'lumpy' in the sense that a power station or a transport system has to be fairly large to be able to provide its services at economically feasible costs. Thus, we have the second version of the balanced-growth theory: this emphasizes the 'technical indivisibilities' in social overhead capital and the need to have a balance between the public utilities providing transport, communications and power on the one hand, and the factories producing consumers' goods on the other, avoiding bottlenecks and excess capacities in the public utilities. In addition to their 'lumpiness', the capital–output ratio in the social overhead services is higher than in most other industries. The aggregate capital requirements of the balanced growth programme of type (2), therefore, are much larger than those of type (1).

Technical indivisibilities in social overhead capital are undoubtedly very important. But even here it is necessary to point out two serious qualifications to the argument that an underdeveloped country cannot start developing unless it is provided beforehand with a complete outfit of transport and communciations, power supply and other social overhead services. First, even in Asia and Africa, different underdeveloped countries already possess these social overhead facilities in varying degrees, depending on their history and geography. For most of these countries, the practical question is not whether to have a complete new outfit of these services starting from scratch, but how much to extend and improve the existing facilities. For instance, the typical choices involved are whether to extend the main railway line or have more feeder lines; whether to extend the road services instead of the railway services; whether to improve existing roads between towns or open up the remoter parts of the country; whether to have smaller power stations combined with wells for irrigation instead of a giant multi-purpose river valley project; and many more. Secondly, even if it is accepted that in the particular circumstances of a country a certain fairly large 'indivisible' social overhead investment is necessary, the fact remains that such a large project cannot be immediately completed to support a simultaneous expansion of consumers' goods industries. A project like this inevitably takes time to construct, and furthermore it is generally capable of being phased for completion over a longer or a shorter period. This possibility of changing the phasing and the time dimension of the project therefore introduces a considerable flexibility to the economic (as distinct from the technical) size of an 'indivisible' social overhead investment. In deciding how quickly a particular large-scale social overhead project should be completed, we should have to compare the costs and inconveniences of putting up with the existing bottlenecks for a time with the extra costs and diseconomies of hurrying up its completion. It may be noted that accelerating the rate of completion of a particular investment project is subject to increasing costs in the same way as increasing the size of a programme for a given period. We may therefore conclude that although the technical indivisibilities in social overhead capital are undoubtedly very important, they are not sufficient to bear the weight of the all-or-nothing approach to economic development suggested by the version (2) of the balanced-growth theory.

(3) The third version of the balanced-growth theory, the 'big push',[1] is nothing short of an attempt to introduce a comprehensive and integrated programme of industrialization, including within its framework not only the consumers' goods industries and social overhead investment but also capital goods industries. The only thing left out there seems to be the agricultural sector. It is argued that in order to launch economic development successfully, it is necessary not only to enlarge the size of the market and obtain the 'internal economies' of large-scale production, but also to obtain the external economies' which arise from simultaneously setting up industries which are technically interdependent with each other; that while these 'technical complementarities' do not normally exist between a horizontal group of consumers' goods industries at the same stage of production, they are very important between a vertical group of

[1] P. N. Rosenstein-Rodan, 'Notes on the theory of the "big push" ', in *Economic Development for Latin America*, Ed. H. S. Ellis, London, 1951.

industries at different stages of production; and that since these external economies are particularly important in the capital goods industries which supply each other and the consumers' goods industries with various inputs in the form of machinery and semi-processed intermediate goods, the capital goods sector should form an integral part of the balanced-growth programme. This comprehensive version of the theory therefore tries to fulfil simultaneously three sets of balanced-growth relations: (a) the horizontal balance between different consumers' goods industries determined by the pattern of expansion in consumers' demand; (b) the balance between social overhead investment and the directly productive activities both in the consumers' and the capital goods sectors; and (c) the vertical balance between the capital goods industries, including the intermediate goods and the consumers' goods industries, determined by the technical complementarities.

Two main features stand out in this version (3) of the theory. The first is the 'external economies' argument: in pursuing this we shall be led to some of the issues involved in the question of the relative importance of planning and free enterprise in promoting economic development in the underdeveloped countries. The second is the argument for comprehensive programming which has been likened to an attempt to impose a complete and brand new 'second floor' on the weak and imperfectly developed one-floor economy of these countries. In examining this argument for comprehensiveness, we shall see the basic weakness of the all-or-nothing approach which is more pronounced in version (3) than in the previous versions.

In welfare economics, 'external economies' are defined as unpaid services which accrue to third parties. These are not fully reflected in private costs and products so that the market prices have to be corrected to take them into account. In the development literature, the concept is used in a different sense. The 'external economies' are the 'pecuniary' economies transmitted through the price system. They originate in a given industry A (say due to the internal economies of overcoming technical indivisibilities) and are then passed on in the form of a lower price for A's product to another industry B which uses it as an input or a factor of production. New investment in A which overcomes its technical indivisibilities will cheapen its product. 'The profits of industry B created by the lower price of factor A, call for investment and expansion in industry B, one result of which will be an increase in industry B's demand for industry A's product. This in its turn will give rise to profits and call for further investment and expansion of industry A.'[1]

Now it is argued that this mutually beneficial type of expansion in output will not take place to the fullest possible extent without a balanced-growth planning. This is so, first, because of the inadequacy of free market prices to act as a signalling device informing private investors about *future* possibilities of expansion in the complementary industries A and B; and secondly because of the imperfect response of private enterprise in the underdeveloped countries to a given signal from the price system. In order to reap the 'external economies' to the full extent, the investment in the two complementary industries would have to be planned together and carried out in an integrated way by a planning authority.

It is true that with an embryonic or imperfectly developed capital market and 'futures' market, the price mechanism in most underdeveloped countries is a very poor signalling system, particularly about future events. But on the other hand, the institutional and administrative machinery available for the governments of the underdeveloped countries is also, with a few exceptions, notoriously weak. It is difficult, therefore, to generalize whether the communication system about future events will always improve with a greater degree of state planning, without taking into account the particular circumstances of each case.

The general problems of coordinating a complex integrated development plan of the type required by version (3) of the balanced-growth theory are well known, and they are frequently thought to be beyond the competence even of the stronger and more efficient governmental machinery of the advanced countries. Two points may however be emphasized. First, the governments of the underdeveloped countries are likely to face their greatest difficulties, not in the initial drawing up of the economic development plans (frequently done with the assistance of foreign experts), but in the execution of the various projects according to a planned time-table and in keeping the different departments and agencies *continually informed* about progress in carrying out the plans. In carrying out a complex set of related projects, there are bound to be various revisions of the original plans, delays and departures from the original time-table. The greater the interdependence between the different components of the plan, the greater the repercussions of an unexpected or un-

[1] T. Scitovsky, 'Two concepts of external economies', *Journal of Political Economy*, April 1954.

avoidable change in one part of the plan on the rest, and the greater the need to keep the different parts of the plans continually revised in the light of the latest available information. These problems of coordination, even within the different parts of the public sector, are formidable, and it is not surprising if 'progress reporting' remains one of the weakest parts of the planning machinery. Secondly, one of the most serious gaps in knowledge required for planning is likely to arise, not merely from a lack of general 'technical know-how' but from ignorance of the local conditions in the underdeveloped countries themselves, and inefficient 'feedback' of this vital local knowledge from the different parts of the country to the central planning machinery. Nor can this be easily remedied, as is commonly supposed, by improving the standard type of statistical information. Frequently local information relevant for efficient planning depends on the qualitative differences and local peculiarities which are abstracted from the statistical compilations concerned with obtaining comparable sets of figures for the country as a whole.

So far we have been concerned with the problems of coordination between the different parts of the government sector. But most underdeveloped countries have a considerable sector in agriculture and consumers' goods industries, traditional and modern; and some countries like India have an important private sector even in the capital goods industries. Thus, in order to assess a comprehensive balanced-growth programme, we have to take into account the rather neglected problem of economic development in the 'mixed economy', viz. the problem or coordination between the government and the private sector. The problem is simpler when the two sectors are complementary; for instance, the government may inform the private sector about its future plans to expand transport and communications or power and may expect the private sector to embark on complementary investment (even here uncertainties about time-tables for the completion of government projects can create difficulties). The problem of coordination and communication becomes formidable when the two sectors are competitive, say either because the government is planning to set up factories to compete with private firms in a given industry or threatening to nationalize private competitors, or because both the government and the private sector are competing for some scarce resources, normally the limited foreign exchange reserves of the country. In this situation, a 'cold war' has developed between the two sectors in many underdeveloped countries. The government departments tend to keep their plans and intentions secret from the private businessmen because they fear 'speculative' activities which will disrupt their plans. On the other hand, private enterprise is inhibited by uncertainties not only about the general economic situation but also about the future intentions of the government and future changes in government regulations. These uncertainties are aggravated when the government, with its drive for a large-scale development plan straining its resources, gets itself into a 'crisis' situation where it is obliged to resort to sudden tightening of controls, notably foreign exchange controls, which upset not only its own plans but also those of the private sector.

Thus, it seems too optimistic to hope that the adoption of comprehensive balanced-growth investment planning by itself, without fundamental improvements in the administrative machinery of the government, and the easing of mutual distrust and suspicion between the government and the private sectors, would improve the efficiency of signalling and coordination between the different sectors of the economy.

Let us now pass on to the question of the responsiveness of private enterprise in underdeveloped countries to a given signal from the price system. Logically, the fact that two industries A and B are complementary does not necessarily mean that they should be expanded simultaneously to reach the maximum possible expansion for both. With the responsiveness of private enterprise, this expansion may be achieved either by expanding A to the full extent and inducing B to expand correspondingly by lowering the price of the input A, or by expanding B to the full extent, inducing A to expand correspondingly under the pressure of excess demand for its product by B. In the advanced countries, this may take place through private initiative only, resulting in what is known as 'vertical integration'. Even in the underdeveloped countries, the state may need to expand through its own initiative either A or B only, rather than both as suggested by the balanced growth theory.

Stressing this possibility, Professor Hirschman has built up an alternative strategy of economic development: the deliberately 'unbalanced growth' approach.[1] He agrees with the balanced-growth theorists about the importance of technical complementarities between industries at different stages of production which he calls 'vertical linkages', but arrives at the opposite conclusion by introducing two further propositions.

[1] A. O. Hirschman, *The Strategy of Economic Development*, New Haven 1958, chs. 3–6.

First, he points out that the degree of complementarity is stronger between some particular groups of industries than others. Thus the aim of development policy should be not to push forward simultaneously on all fronts as though these complementarities were uniformly distributed all over the economy, but to select and concentrate on particular 'strategic' sectors of the economy where these interdependent linkage effects may be expected to be strongest. He believes that these strategic parts of the economy are to be found where the network of input–output relationships is thickest, representing industries which buy the largest part of their inputs from other industries, or sell the largest part of their outputs to other industries (as distinct from the final consumers), or both.

Secondly, he argues that the balanced growth approach, even if it were successful, will merely achieve a once-for-all increase in national income, coming to rest at a higher plateau representing the balanced-growth equilibrium. Economic development, however, should be a continuous dynamic process, kept alive by the tensions of shortages and excess supplies and by the disequilibria in the strategic sectors which are capable of responding to these pace-setting pressures. The balanced-growth theorists would like the two complementary industries A and B to expand simultaneously to their 'full' equilibrium level which would exhaust the external economies possible in the initial situation. Professor Hirschman would like either A or B to overshoot the equilibrium point. He hopes that the resulting pressures of excess demand or excess supply would change the initial situation itself and lead to further economic development in a series of 'leap-frogging' movements.

The whole question depends to a large extent on the assumption we make about the responsiveness of private enterprise in the underdeveloped countries to a disequilibrium situation with profitable opportunities of increasing investment. The balanced growth theorists are thinking of a situation where the complementary industries are new industries requiring a considerable initial outlay of capital and technical experience on the part of the new entrants into them. They feel that it is beyond the capacity of unaided private enterprise in the underdeveloped countries to respond effectively to this situation so that the government must take the initiative in launching a balanced growth programme. There are, however, considerable differences among the balanced growth theorists themselves over the question how much of the programme should be directly carried by the government planning authority. Some are content merely to point out the theoretical advantages of the balanced-growth approach without specifying the exact proportion of the 'mixed economy'. Others are contemptuous about 'patching up the market' and imply that the bulk of the balanced-growth programme, not only in the social overhead capital but also in the capital and the consumers' goods sectors, should be carried out by state enterprise.

The popular argument concerning the shortage of entrepreneurs in the underdeveloped countries, however, is not a sufficient reason for increasing the government sector. For if the private sector suffers from a shortage of entrepreneurs, the government sector will equally suffer from a shortage of administrators who can perform these entre-preneurial functions. As Professor Hirschman has pointed out, the balanced-growth approach makes an impossible demand on the underdeveloped countries by requiring them to provide, all at once, entrepreneurs and managers to run a whole flock of new industries; if they could do this, they would not be underdeveloped in the first place. But he believes that the problem of increasing the supply of entrepreneurs and capital can be solved in the long run, provided the right type of pressures are used to bring them forth. He believes that, if suitable investment opportunities are opened up by his unbalanced-growth approach, additional supplies of domestic savings will be forthcoming, and that what is holding back many underdeveloped countries is not so much the shortage of savings as the 'ability to invest'. Similarly, the unbalanced-growth approach may be regarded as providing a school for entrepreneurs, spelling out their profit opportunities in block letters by means of deliberately engineered bottlenecks and excess capacities, and thus assisting the 'learning process' of the potential entrepreneurs in the underdeveloped countries.

The limitations of the balanced-growth and the unbalanced-growth approaches in the setting of international trade will be considered in Chapter 9. For the moment, I shall conclude this chapter by pointing out the basic weakness of the all-or-nothing approach which version (3) of the balanced-growth theory suffers from more than the previous versions. The crucial practical question which faces the developing countries is not how to plan their development programmes as though they had unlimited supplies of resources, but what sort of choices they should make when their currently available resources are insufficient for a comprehensive balanced-growth programme. The question of having to make unpalatable choices has been pushed into the back-ground, first by the assumption of the 'unlimited supply of labour' and second by the expectation of greater foreign aid. In the previous chapter, we have already seen that the cushion provided by the economic potential from 'disguised unemployment' is very thin. So now the main reliance has to be placed on greater foreign aid. But however generous the supply of foreign aid, it can only relieve the harshness of choices rather than abolish the basic economic problem of having to make choices. This is particularly true when it is remembered that in many underdeveloped countries the basic 'scarce factor' may not be the shortage of saving but the ability to absorb and invest capital effectively. It is the basic weakness of the various versions of the balanced growth theories that they obscure this problem of choice. The more comprehensive the minimum size of the development programme they advocate, the more the problem of choice is obscured.

For instance, the version (1) obscures the choices within the consumers' goods sector, but at an overall level the choice it makes is clear. If the underdeveloped countries do not have enough resources to push ahead on all fronts, they should concentrate on investment in consumers' goods industries, assuming the necessary capital goods can be imported through trade or aid. This choice is made on the basis that the limitation in the size of the market is the most important obstacle to economic development, and that the existing levels of consumption are so low that it is better to try to raise consumption immediately even at the cost of a slower rate of economic growth in the future. The converse of version (1), the 'communist model' of industrialization, also makes a clear-cut choice, in favour of the capital goods sector. This is done presumably on the basis that the most important requirement for economic development is to be able to reap the technical economies of scale and complementarities, and that since these are most abundant in the capital goods sector, it is better to sacrifice present consumption for the sake of the faster rate of future economic growth. The 'big push' or version (3) of the balanced-growth theory, however, insists on expanding investment, not only in the consumers' goods industries, but in the capital goods industries and also in the public utilities and social overhead capital. By insisting on this simultaneous expansion on all fronts, it has not only evaded the crucial economic choices between present and future income, but has frequently encouraged many underdeveloped countries to push too far beyond their currently available resources and organizing ability. This is frequently defended on the grounds that it might elicit more foreign aid. It is questionable, however, whether the prospect of foreign aid, which is far from certain, is sufficient to justify pushing the developing countries into a 'crisis' situation in which they are no longer in a position to make any coherent or consistent choices and are merely driven from one *ad hoc* emergency measure to another. This is surely the reverse of 'economic planning'.

8

THE PATH OF BALANCED GROWTH AND
THE RATE OF ECONOMIC DEVELOPMENT

Let us now turn from the *size* to the *path* of balanced growth. Instead of the minimum size of the balanced-growth programme required to start economic development successfully, I am now concerned with the rate of economic development which can be sustained over a period of time, by expanding the output of the different sectors of the economy in a balanced-growth relation. The exponents of the balanced-growth path theory, notably Professors Lewis and Nurkse,[1] explicitly regard agriculture also as one of the 'industries' to be included in the balanced-growth framework. Thus, while the previous versions of the theory were mainly concerned with the balanced growth within the manufacturing sector only, emphasis has now shifted to the broad inter-sectoral balance between agriculture and manufactures, each sector providing the market and supplying the necessary ingredients for the expansion of the other. The balanced-growth path theory, therefore, may be looked upon as two-edged criticism, both of the orthodox view that the underdeveloped countries should specialize in primary export production for which they have a comparative advantage, and of the modern view that they should embark on an all-out drive for industrialization.

The conflict between international specialization and internal balanced growth will be discussed in the next chapter. For the moment, I shall concentrate on the internal and domestic aspects of the balanced-growth path in relation to industrialization and the

[1] W. A. Lewis, *Theory of Economic Growth*, London 1959, pp. 276–83; R. Nurkse, *The Conflict Between 'Balanced Growth' and International Specialization*, Ankara 1957, and *Patterns of Trade and Development*, Wicksell Lectures 1959, Stockholm 1959.

rate of economic development, and in the setting of the overpopulated underdeveloped countries.

Industrialization is popularly regarded as synonymous with economic development by the people of the developing countries. They feel that agriculture is an inherently less productive occupation than manufacturing industry,[1] and that the present economic structure of their countries, characterized by a large proportion of the total working force in primary production, is somehow lop-sided and unbalanced and should be cured by an all-out drive for manufacturing industry. It is not unfair to say that this bias in favour of industrialization seems to be shared even by the economists who advocate the 'balanced-growth' approach of the type we have examined in the last chapter, with its emphasis on balanced growth only within the manufacturing sector. This bias for manufacturing industry seems to arise partly out of a desire to find something which can absorb the rural surplus labour and partly out of the feeling that, before the developing countries can proceed along the balanced-growth path, their initial imbalance between agriculture and manufacturing industry must be cured by starting with a counterbalancing expansion of the manufacturing industry.

The bottleneck in agriculture

Some of the weaknesses in the argument for a one-sided drive to expand the manufacturing sector can be seen once we try to apply the balanced-growth path approach systematically. To begin with, it is not possible to say that there is an 'imbalance' between agriculture and industry in an underdeveloped country simply because the larger proportion of its labour and other resources is employed in agriculture. What is relevant is not the present proportion of *resources* in the two sectors but the future rate of expansion in the *output* of the two sectors. In a closed economy, the fact that a larger proportion of its labour is employed in agriculture does mean that productivity in

[1] This belief may also derive from statistical correlations showing that while countries with high per capita incomes have a larger proportion of their labour in secondary and tertiary industries, countries with low per capita incomes have a larger proportion of their labour in primary production. What is not always clearly understood is that the higher proportion of labour in secondary and tertiary industries may be the consequence and not the cause of higher per capita incomes, reflecting the well-known tendency of people to spend more on manufactures and services and less on food as their income rises. For further discussion of this subject see P. T. Bauer and B. S. Yamey, 'Economic progress and occupational distribution', *Economic Journal*, December 1951.

agriculture is low and that it requires a large number of workers in agriculture to support a non-agricultural worker in the rest of the economy. But this cannot be cured simply by trying to transfer labour from agriculture to manufacturing. Indeed, this transfer will not be possible unless the productivity of the agricultural sector is raised simultaneously, enabling it to feed a larger number of industrial workers. A reduction in the overcrowding on land may be necessary as a method of facilitating the improvement in agricultural productivity. But the essential point is that the manufacturing sector cannot continue to expand for long without a balanced expansion in the output of the agricultural sector. Given the logic of the balanced-growth path, the rate of development of the whole economy will be determined by the rate of expansion in its slowest moving component part; and given the tendency to diminishing returns, agriculture clearly qualifies for this role as the major bottleneck. Thus, even if the manufacturing sector can import the durable capital goods from abroad, its rate of expansion will ultimately depend on the rate of expansion in the output of the agricultural sector.

In Chapter 6 we have seen that rural overpopulation characterized by the 'zero marginal product of labour' does not automatically ensure that the 'disguised unemployment' can be removed without reducing the total agricultural output and therefore that there would be a food surplus waiting to be mobilized to feed non-agricultural workers. With given agricultural techniques, total output will remain unchanged only on condition that the same total amount of work continues to be applied to the land. This means that those who are left behind on the land after the surplus workers are removed must somehow be induced to put in the extra work to maintain the same total volume of work as before. This question assumes a dominating importance when we are concerned not merely with maintaining a particular total agricultural output and a once-for-all transfer of the food surplus but with trying to have a continually expanding food surplus from the agricultural sector to feed the expanding labour force in the manufacturing sector.

There are two main approaches to the problem of expanding the output of the agricultural sector. On the one hand, there are positive economic incentives to induce the farmers to expand their marketable surplus. This requires that an expanding stream of manufactured consumers' goods should be available, on attractive terms, for exchange with the agricultural produce. Thus, the crucial balanced-growth relationship in this context will be between the agricultural sector and the consumers' goods manufacturing sector. This approximates to the version (1) of the balanced-growth theory in the last chapter. On the other hand, we may rely mainly on the provision of capital goods such as irrigation, power and machinery, and of other inputs such as fertilizers and improved seeds to expand agricultural output. Depending on the type of technical complementarity we stress, the crucial balanced growth-relationship will be either between agriculture and social overhead investment (as in the version (2)) or between agriculture and the capital goods sector approximating to what I termed the 'communist' model in the last chapter.

Formally, the difference between the two approaches appears to be that the first stresses the interdependence on the demand side and the second stresses the interdependence on the supply side. But more fundamental differences are involved in emphasizing the balanced growth between agriculture and the consumers' goods sector as contrasted with that between agriculture and the capital goods sector. They involve different attitudes towards the use of positive economic incentives or the use of compulsive economic pressures; and towards present consumption or the future rate of economic growth.

If we are thinking of using positive economic incentives to induce the farmers to produce a larger marketable surplus of agriculture, then the conventional distinction between 'consumers' goods' and 'capital goods' is rather blurred. In so far as food is necessary for the expansion of the manufacturing sector, it is as much a 'capital good' as durable machinery: the classical concept of capital as the 'subsistence fund' required to maintain the workers during a time-involving process of production is still applicable. But granted this, the supply of manufactured consumers' goods which is necessary in order to induce the farmers to produce a larger marketable surplus of food may be regarded as much a 'capital good' as the direct physical inputs into agriculture. This is of course not to deny the importance of the essential physical inputs and capital goods in increasing agricultural output; but only to point out that the mere physical provision of these inputs and capital goods need not result in a larger supply of food surplus unless economic incentives are created for the farmers to make full use of them. Hence the crucial importance of the balanced growth between agriculture and the manufactured consumers' goods sector.

Those who favour the second approach will argue, however, that to try to expand the output of the agricultural sector by using purely positive economic incentives may not be effective and is a very socially costly approach for a poor country. In trying to offer economic incentives, we are merely acquiescing in the farmers' unwillingness to postpone present consumption for the sake of faster future economic growth. With the limited resources of the manufacturing sector, expansion of the consumers' goods sector can take place only at the expense of the capital goods sector. Since economies of scale and technical complementarities are more important in the capital goods sector than in the consumers' goods sector, the attempt to maintain a balanced growth on the demand side between agriculture and the consumers' goods sector will therefore slow down the overall growth rate of the economy. They would prefer a considerable use of negative pressures to make a forcible collection of the agricultural surplus through taxation or compulsory collection of produce combined with the provision of the necessary inputs such as fertilizers, seeds or irrigation, for example.

In so far as we can judge from the experiences of the underdeveloped countries, neither the first nor the second approach is likely to succeed on its own, and the practical problem is to try to find an effective combination of the two which will suit local circumstances. In Chapter 3, we have seen that peasants do respond vigorously to positive economic incentives, but, under conditions of unaided free market conditions, much of the expansion in their output has been the result of bringing more land under cultivation rather than of improving agricultural productivity. On the other hand, the overpopulated countries can only expand their agricultural output by improving their agricultural productivity. In order to bring about changes in agricultural techniques and organization, the incentive approach needs to be supplemented by a variety of other measures ranging from improvements in irrigation and transport, in agricultural credit, marketing and extension services, to the provision of fertilizers and improved seeds. But this does not mean that a forcible extraction of the agricultural surplus through taxation or compulsory collection of agricultural produce on the 'communist' model is likely to work. This method has not been particularly successful even in Soviet Russia which in contrast to the overpopulated countries of today started out as a considerable exporter of wheat and still has a considerable amount of unused land. A country like India simply does not possess an 'agricultural surplus' in the Russian sense which may be forcibly collected. All we have got is the optical illusion of the 'concealed saving potential' based on the misconception that, because the marginal product of labour in overcrowded subsistence agriculture is zero, the surplus labour can be removed without reducing total output, thus automatically creating a food surplus to be extracted by taxation and compulsion. But as we have seen, the total agricultural output is likely to decline unless those who are left behind on the land are given positive economic incentives to work harder and to adopt more productive methods of cultivation. It is not inconceivable that beyond a certain point the attempt to pursue a forcible method of collecting the agricultural surplus may well drive the peasants into producing no surplus at all.

A more promising way in which a combination of government action and market incentives may be used to increase the agricultural production of a densely populated country is shown by Japan. This is for the government to promote research and development of better agricultural methods of a labour-intensive and land-saving character. Thus, while agricultural development in the newly settled countries with abundant land and labour scarcity such as the United States was characterized by labour-saving innovations in the form of progressive mechanization of agriculture, the Japanese agricultural development was based on research and development in a different direction: it was characterized by high-yielding seeds, intensive application of fertilizer and a systematic provision of irrigation facilities. These combined to raise the productivity of land while encouraging the intensive application of labour to small peasant holdings. The provision of irrigation facilities enabled the peasants to reap not only the full productive potentialities of the improved seeds and fertilizer, but also to increase the number of crops which could be grown on the same plot of land each year. Thus, starting from the conditions of technically backward peasant agriculture and population pressure on land, the Japanese agricultural output increased in a spectacular way. The rice yield per hectare steadily rose from around $2\frac{1}{2}$ metric tons in the 1890s to 5 tons in the 1960s. The government activities in promoting agricultural research, in spreading the knowledge about improved agriculture and in the provision of irrigation facilities were combined with the use of the market incentives. In particular, there was a steady cheapening of the fertilizer relative to the price of rice received by the farmers which encouraged the adoption of the new agricultural technology.[1]

The Japanese model of agricultural development has already been successfully transferred to Taiwan and South Korea, countries having

[1] Y. Hayami and V. W. Ruttan, *Agricultural Development: An International Perspective*, Baltimore, Maryland 1971, pt. III.

some of the highest population densities in Asia. By the latter half of the 1960s, new technological advances had spread the seed-and-ferti-lizer revolution—now known as the 'Green Revolution'—to South-East Asian countries and to India and Pakistan.

Since India is regarded as the prototype of an overpopulated country struggling at the minimum subsistence level it is necessary to touch briefly on her post-war agricultural development. Even before the dramatic advent of the 'Green Revolution' Indian agri-cultural production both of food grains and other crops was growing at a somewhat faster rate than is popularly assumed. During the period 1950–65, Indian agricultural production grew about 3·6% per annum—faster than her population growth of 2·5% per annum. But the picture is complicated by the uneven rate of growth of agricultural output between the different states, Punjab, Gujarat and Madras states showing the fastest rates of growth. A notable factor which has contributed to this growth appears to be the rise of com-mercial and even 'capitalist' agriculture on larger holdings, using improved methods of cultivation, wage labour and a greater use of irrigation facilities, both those provided by the government and those provided by privately-owned tube-wells. The advent of the 'Green Revolution' and the introduction of the new high-yielding varieties of rice and wheat has accelerated the trend towards rising agricultural productivity and towards the larger-scale commercialized farming. It is, however, still an open question whether India will become self-sufficient in food with the further spread of the 'Green Revolution'. For one thing, the 'Green Revolution' should not be regarded as a once-for-all technical breakthrough but a continuing process of research and development, and there are many technical problems which remain to be solved, such as the adaptation of the new varieties of seeds to local agricultural conditions. For another, the technical success of the 'Green Revolution' has accentuated many organiza-tional and economic problems, such as storage, transport, marketing and agricultural credit. The provision of adequate irrigation facilities to some regions may also require large capital investments. Currently, in spite of her progress in increasing agricultural production, India still seems to be vulnerable to unfavourable weather conditions and is obliged to import large quantities of food during years of bad harvest.[1]

[1] For a brief survey of post-war Indian agricultural development, see E. A. G. Robinson, 'Economic progress in India', *Three Banks Review*, March 1970, reprinted in *Aspects of Indian Economic Development*, Ed. P. Chaudhuri, London 1971.

Choice of techniques and the choice between present and future

So far, we have been considering the choice between present consumption and future rate of growth in terms of the choice between expanding the consumers' goods sector or the capital goods sector to stimulate corresponding expansion in the agricultural sector. But even when it is decided how much of the different types of goods should be produced, the problem of choice between the different time-paths of the income stream still remains. It now appears in the form of the choice between different methods of producing the same type of goods. Thus, in an overpopulated country suffering from a shortage of capital and land, should we not always choose the most labour-intensive method of producing a given commodity which combines the greatest possible quantity of the abundant factor— labour—to a given unit of scarce factor—capital or land? Under what conditions should we depart from this apparently common-sensical rule? Part of the answer to this question depends on our choice between present and future consumption.

To some extent, the question of the correct choice of techniques stated in terms of two factors of production such as labour and capital is oversimplified and artificial. In an actual situation, the choice depends not only on two selected factors but on a variety of other things, notably the third main factor—skilled labour. Many underdeveloped countries suffer from a greater shortage of skills than of material capital, so that they sometimes prefer more expensive machinery, which reduces repairs and maintenance, to cheaper or second-hand machinery which, although it might reduce the ratio of capital to unskilled labour, requires a larger amount of the scarcest factor, skilled labour. Similarly, the machines which the underdeveloped countries can import are designed for the conditions in the advanced countries and are frequently too complicated and labour-saving for their own requirements. But these machines are produced in large numbers according to standard specifications and to try to alter them to suit the local conditions in the underdeveloped countries may make them a great deal more expensive than the standard article. Thus, in a wide range of modern manufacturing industry, the underdeveloped countries may have little choice but to buy the standard machines which are available in the market and, in most cases, to employ foreign technicians to run them. All they can do, in suitable cases, is to try to have multiple shifts of labour on a particular machine.

In spite of this, however, it is instructive to study the problem of the choice of techniques in relation to an overpopulated country such as India. For this has relevance not only to the relation between labour-intensive handicraft industries and modern factories in the consumers' goods sector, but also to the different methods of providing social overhead capital such as irrigation and transport. And, most interestingly in the light of my previous analysis, it has relevance also to the question of change-over from subsistence to commercial agriculture. Furthermore, the question of the choice of techniques leads us via the choice between present consumption and future economic growth to the equally fundamental choice between greater economic equality and faster economic growth.

At the end of Chapter 6, I said that beyond the problem of finding the total capital requirements to produce a target output of a particular commodity on the basis of a given sectoral capital–output ratio, it is necessary to consider whether this ratio represents the most economical way of producing this commodity. At first sight, it may appear that to economize capital, we have merely to compare the different capital–output ratios required in the different methods of producing the same commodity, and choose the method with the lowest capital–output ratio. This is of course another way of saying that we should pick the method which produces the highest value of output per unit of capital. But this ignores the fact that, in addition to capital, labour is required to produce the commodity. So to find out the net value of output per unit of capital, we should take the gross value of output, and deduct the total labour cost of that output—measuring the total labour costs by the number of labour units required multiplied by the given money wage rate.

I can now state the bare bones of the problem of the choice of techniques. Some methods of producing a particular commodity are labour-intensive—they require a large quantity of labour in combination with a given unit of capital. But because of this, the labour costs in these methods are relatively high and they may therefore yield a comparatively low net output per unit of capital after the labour costs are deducted. These methods are typified by the handicraft and cottage industry methods of producing consumers' goods, and the spade-and-bucket method of constructing roads and irrigation works. On the other hand, there are the capital-intensive or labour-saving methods of producing a particular commodity, typified by the modern factory methods of producing consumers' goods, and mechanized methods of constructing roads, irrigation works and other projects. Here, because of lower labour costs and higher productivity, the net output per unit of capital may be comparatively high.

The advantage of the more labour-intensive techniques is that for a given amount of capital investment they create a larger volume of employment. Since most of the wage income is spent on consumption, there is therefore a higher level of present consumption. Since a large volume of employment means that the available income is spread over a larger number of people, there is also a higher degree of economic equality. On the other hand, the advantage of the more capital-intensive methods is, that for a given amount of capital investment, they yield a higher net output or surplus above the wage bill; this surplus can be made available for further investment. So although they yield a lower volume of present employment and consumption, they promise a higher rate of economic growth in the future, and therefore a higher potential level of employment and consumption in the future. There is, however, a greater degree of unequal distribution of income between the (state or private) 'capitalists' who obtain the surplus and the wage earners, and also between those workers who obtain immediate employment and those who for the present are left unabsorbed in the productive process.

The upshot of recent discussions on the choice of techniques has been to show that it is not possible to make an invariable choice in favour of more labour-intensive techniques even in overpopulated countries, unless we make explicit choices between present and future. The more we value raising the present level of consumption and employment against future growth, the more we should favour labour-intensive techniques. The 'commonsense' view that overpopulated countries should always prefer labour-intensive methods conceals an implicit preference for present over future, and represents a very short 'planning horizon'. On the longer 'planning horizon', the more we value the future rate of growth over the present level of consumption and employment, the more we should favour capital-intensive methods which are capable of yielding a larger surplus of output over wage costs for a given capital outlay and so make possible a higher rate of re-investment for the future.

However, this simple conclusion needs to be modified when the analysis is extended to the problem of the choice of techniques in agriculture. Here we have two types of capital goods—those which are substitutes for labour such as tractors and those which are substitutes for land, such as irrigation works. Broadly speaking, investment in the first type of capital goods is equivalent to an increase in the supply of labour: thus investment in mechanized farming creates a new source of labour power which reduces the need to employ human labour. Similarly, investment in the second type of capital goods is equivalent to an increase in the supply of land: irrigation and the use of improved seeds and fertilizer which increases the productivity of land or increases the number of crops which can be grown in succession on the same piece of land is equivalent to an increase in the supply of land. Thus for the underdeveloped countries with heavy population pressure on land the obvious course to follow would be to invest as much as possible in the land-saving type of capital—in irrigation, improved seeds and fertilizer—and to invest as little as possible in labour-saving in mechanized farming.[1]

This suggests certain guidelines for the choice between three different types of agriculture suggested by various proposals for land reform.

First, there is the proposal to break up the larger estates and to redistribute land in small plots to the landless peasants for subsistence farming. It is frequently suggested that to prevent the 'alienation' of land from the peasants there should be legal prohibitions on the sale or renting of the distributed land. This type of land reform, which amounts to the preservation of the traditional subsistence type of farming, would have the effect of providing the greatest volume of employment, 'disguised' or otherwise, for a given area of land. Since labour is free within the family, it will be applied to maximize the total output which can be squeezed out of land, i.e. up to the point at which its marginal product is reduced to zero. With given techniques, this type of agriculture can support the largest number of people on a given area of land. But the attempt to preserve the traditional social framework from the effects of commercialization is likely to lead to agricultural stagnation, aggravated by population pressure. Thus while it may maximize present levels of consumption it offers nothing for future growth.

Second, there is the proposal to maintain the small-scale labour-intensive system of peasant agriculture while encouraging the process of commercialization, not only in the growing of cash crops but also in the employment of wage labour and in the freedom to sell, purchase and rent land. With the development of an agricultural labour market the commercialization of agriculture would tend to reduce the labour-intensity per unit of land, even on the basis of the least

[1] A. K. Sen, *Choice of Techniques*, 3rd ed., Oxford 1968. See ch. 1 and Appendix A.

mechanized method of farming, using draught animals. This is so because the employer of wage labour would apply it to land only up to the point where its marginal product is equal to the wage rate. Given the opportunity for wage employment even the family supply of labour will also be applied to the family farm only up to the point where its marginal product is equal to the wage rate in the neighbourhood. Beyond this point it would be more profitable to divert some part of family labour to wage employment. Thus the introduction of a wage system would reduce the total employment and output from a given area of land compared with subsistence agriculture, given the same agricultural techniques. But commercial agriculture has the advantage of providing a marketable food surplus above the retained consumption on the farm which can be sent to any part of the economy where it is most needed—to feed the workers in the manufácturing sector or those producing social overhead capital. Further, commercial agriculture is likely to be more efficient and yield a larger total output than subsistence farming, since a part of the cash income from it can be used for better seeds, fertilizer or in the installation of tube-wells for irrigation purposes.

Third, there is the proposal to consolidate small and fragmented peasant plots with larger-scale 'collective' or 'capitalist' farms suitable for highly mechanized methods of farming, using tractors. The proposal to introduce such a highly capital-intensive and labour-saving method of agriculture has been advocated on the ground that it would produce the largest amount of agricultural surplus over and above the consumption of agricultural labour and the re-investment of this surplus would lead to a faster future rate of growth.

For the densely populated underdeveloped countries, the second type of agriculture seems to be clearly more suitable than the first or the third. As we have seen, the Japanese pattern of agricultural development based on the improved seed-and-fertilizer technology does not offer any significant economies of scale and can be efficiently practised on small peasant holdings. Nevertheless, in some parts of India and Pakistan there is a tendency for the larger 'capitalist' farmers to adopt the highly capital-intensive and labour-saving 'modern' farming, using heavy tractors. This has been encouraged by the excessively favourable terms on which the larger farmers, like the larger enterprises in the manufacturing sector, are able to obtain capital and foreign exchange. Thus inappropriate interest rate and exchange-rate policies have aggravated the 'dualism' not only in manufactures but also in agriculture. The scarce capital resources which could have been used in the land-saving type of investment have been used instead in the labour-saving type of investment, increasing the problem of unemployment.

Forced saving and deficit financing

I shall now return to the central issues of the balanced-growth path theory. We have seen that the overall rate of growth for the economy will be determined by the rate of growth of its slowest moving sector, agriculture. To try to stimulate the output of the agricultural sector by using only positive economic incentives may be effective, but this means diverting a considerable part of the resources of the manu-facturing sector from the capital goods sector to the consumers' goods sector, and slowing down the rate of growth. On the other hand, however, to try to use negative pressures such as taxation or com-pulsory collection of produce may also lead to a 'peasants' strike', resulting in a lesser amount of agricultural surplus, and slowing down the rate of growth. In this situation, many economists have toyed with the idea of accelerating economic growth by deficit financing which would facilitate the transfer of 'disguised unemployment' from agriculture into productive work, particularly in the construction of social overhead capital such as irrigation projects or roads. They also argue that this type of deficit financing may be pursued without serious long-term consequences since the inflation which it creates will be 'self-destroying'—because when the capital projects are com-pleted they will add to the output of agriculture and other con-sumers' goods.

This is altogether different from saying that the social cost of making use of the 'disguised unemployment' is zero. On the con-trary, it is recognized that there is a genuine social cost in doing so in the form of extra consumption by the workers on the capital projects, who will spend most of their wages on food and other consumers' goods. In fact, deficit financing is called for because this extra consumption cannot be met out of taxation and voluntary saving, so that 'forced saving' has to be imposed through inflation. So while the workers on the capital projects are able to command a larger share of real income through the increase in money incomes, the farmers, for instance, will find that they have been obliged to cut down their level of consumption through the rise in the prices of the consumers' goods that they wish to buy.

The idea that inflation will be self-destroying is based on the assumption that the extra money income created by deficit financing will become *stabilized* at a certain level, so that after a time-lag, the extra output of consumers' goods which results from the new capital goods can catch up with it.[1] This in turn is based on the Keynesian Multiplier theory and the assumption of stable marginal propensity to save and consume. In the original Keynesian context, we start from a situation of depression where both labour and the productive capacity which goes with it are unemployed. Deficit financing, therefore, will merely expand employment and output without raising prices of consumers' goods whose output can be expanded directly. Given stable prices, then it is reasonable to assume that at each round the people who receive the extra income will go on saving and spending in certain stable proportions as before; and so long as a certain proportion of income is saved each round—that is, so long as the marginal propensity to consume is less than 1—then the total resultant income will converge towards a stable equilibrium level. In the underdeveloped countries, however, we start from a situation with only surplus labour without the necessary productive equipment to go with it. So surplus labour can at best produce some extra capital goods which only after a time-lag can produce consumers' goods. Immediately, therefore, the prices of consumers' goods must go up. How far this inflation will be self-destroying depends on how far the people in the underdeveloped countries who receive the extra money income will go on saving and spending it in stable proportions in the face of the rising prices of consumers' goods.

In the underdeveloped countries which have just emerged from the orthodox monetary conditions typified by the 100% Sterling Standard, people may still retain some confidence in money and hold to the 'illusion' that its value will continue to be the same as before. The posthumous benefit of this maligned orthodox monetary system is that it provides the newly independent monetary authorities with some scope for deficit financing without upsetting confidence. But as prices continue to rise, the marginal propensity to consume, which started very high in any case, will tend towards 1. For one thing, rising costs of living will compel people to spend most of their income and reduce their saving, and even borrow for consumption purposes. For another thing, as soon as people expect that prices will go on rising, they will become increasingly disinclined to save any part of their money income, since this form of saving will be quickly depreciating in value. They will increasingly tend to spend all their

[1] W. A. Lewis, 'Economic development with unlimited supplies of labour', *The Manchester School*, May 1954.

money income as quickly as possible by hoarding food and other consumers' goods, or by buying gold, jewellery and real estate whose value keeps up with rising prices.   Once this gathers momentum, money incomes will not be stabilized at a certain level in the Keynesian manner; instead we shall be back in the world of the quantity theory where the total volume of purchasing power is increased at each round as the original sum of money is multiplied by its quickening velocity of circulation.   The rising cost of living will lead to demands for higher money wages, and if they are conceded we shall have the familiar wage-price spiral.   In these conditions it seems very difficult to believe that inflation will be self-destroying, and this pessimism is confirmed by the typical monetary conditions in underdeveloped countries which are marked by the continual tendency to boil over into further bouts of rising prices or tighter foreign exchange controls to meet the balance-of-payments crises.[1]

To sum up: there is no simple short cut to increasing the agricultural surplus without trying to tackle the difficult problem of raising agricultural productivity.   The merit of the balanced-growth path theory is to show that the overall rate of growth of a (closed) economy cannot be sustained without a simultaneous expansion in its slowest moving sector—agriculture.   This basic 'balanced-growth' relation arises from the fact that the size of the agricultural surplus forms the 'subsistence fund' required to support the workers during the waiting period before the result of their labour becomes available in the form of final output. The larger the size of its agricultural surplus, the longer a society can afford to wait for the fruits of capital investment, and the more elaborate the type of capital investment it can afford to undertake.   The role of the *marketable* surplus is that it helps to move the food surplus of the farms to other parts of the economy where it may be able to contribute more to future economic growth.   It is the tragedy of the overpopulated countries that while they need a faster rate of growth to relieve population pressure, they have a smaller potential food surplus above minimum subsistence consumption to be used for this purpose. If they are too poor to rely on positive economic incentives to induce the farmers to grow more food, they do not possess a large potential agricultural surplus which can be extracted by coercive methods, by taxation and by forced saving.   A more promising approach shown by the

[1] cf. M. Bronfenbrenner, 'The high cost of economic development', *Land Economics*, August 1953.

Japanese model of agricultural development is the research and development of the land-saving and labour-using type of agricultural improvements which in combination with appropriate economic incentives to the farmers would increase the size of the marketable agricultural surplus.

9

INTERNATIONAL TRADE AND
ECONOMIC DEVELOPMENT

The assumption of the closed economy which I have been using to examine the theory of balanced growth in the preceding two chapters is a rather restrictive framework for the study of the underdeveloped countries. Most of these countries are small countries with limited domestic markets. International trade has to play an important, frequently a dominant, role in their economic development. But once we introduce international trade, it is no longer necessary for a country to maintain an internal balanced-growth relation between the different sectors of its domestic economy. It may produce some commodities in excess of its domestic demand and export them, and in return import other commodities for which its domestic demand exceeds domestic production. Indeed, it is the aim of the standard international trade theory to show that correcting domestic imbalances through exports and imports is generally preferable to maintaining a strict balanced-growth relationship within a self-sufficient economy, since the country can now enjoy the advantages of international specialization according to its comparative costs.

This traditional free-trade doctrine has been received with distrust and hostility in most underdeveloped countries. At a semi-popular but influential level, the antagonistic attitude towards free international trade may be traced to a number of powerful sentiments. First, there is the reaction against the 'colonial' or nineteenth-century pattern of international division of labour under which the underdeveloped countries specialized in the production of primary exports. Related to it is the identification of economic development with the growth of manufacturing industry and the belief that the mainspring for economic development can be provided only by a policy of promoting domestic industrialization. Third, there is the general distrust of the market forces and the reliance on government planning to promote economic development. This is strengthened by a desire to use economic planning as a protective shell to insulate the domestic economy from the disturbing influences of outside economic forces which might undermine national 'economic independence'.

At a more technical level, the various arguments put forward against free trade and export expansion and for domestic industrialization and import substitution fall into two main groups. First there are the arguments alleging unfavourable world market demand conditions facing the exports from the underdeveloped countries: the world market demand for primary products, it is argued, is not only highly unstable in the short run but is also likely to be inelastic and stagnant in the long run. Second, there are the arguments justifying the protection of domestic manufacturing industry in the underdeveloped countries: these include the argument based on 'disguised unemployment'; the 'infant industry' argument; and the argument that manufacturing industry would provide dynamic impetus to economic development through various 'linkages'. I shall examine these arguments by turn.

Short-run instability of demand for primary exports

A majority of underdeveloped countries are small countries with a high ratio of exports to the national income; moreover, a number of them are dependent on the export of a few primary products. During the Great Depression of the 1930s, most of them suffered the traumatic experience of a catastrophic decline in their export incomes. Given the broad background, it had seemed eminently plausible to argue that the underdeveloped countries should be extremely wary of trying to increase their specialization in primary exports because this would increase their vulnerability to short-run fluctuations in the world market demand for these products, which appears to be more unstable than that for the manufactured products. Until recently most economists have implicitly accepted this view and have exercised their minds with the difficult and intractable task of organizing effective and acceptable commodity stabilization schemes as a method of reducing the vulnerability of the underdeveloped countries to short-run fluctuations in the world market demand for primary products. It was feared that this short-run instability would make it difficult not only to maintain a stable level of consumption and living standards in the underdeveloped countries but also to maintain a stable level of investment for their long-run development.

Recent systematic studies of the available facts of the situation have however suggested that these fears have been exaggerated. First, it has been shown that the division of world exports into 'primary products' and 'manufactured products' is too crude to reveal any clear differences in the degree of instability, and that instability is more pronounced for capital goods than for consumer goods cutting across the conventional dichotomy between primary and manufactured products. (Moreover, as we have noted in Chapter 2, it is not adequate to identify primary exporters with the underdeveloped countries, since a number of advanced countries are important primary exporters.) Second, it has been shown that fluctuations in the export receipts from primary products are made up of two components: fluctuations in the price originating from world market conditions and fluctuations in the physical volume of output originating in the domestic conditions of the exporting countries, and that frequently the fluctuation in the volume of output is a more important factor in causing the fluctuation in the export receipts. In so far as this is true, the attempt to stabilize the price of the exports without being able to stabilize the physical volume of exports may have a destabilizing effect on the export receipts. Thirdly, it has been shown that because of the high marginal propensity to import in the underdeveloped countries, the 'foreign-trade multiplier' is small, i.e. fluctuations in exports have a small effect on the fluctuations in the level of domestic income; and further, that there is only a weak relationship between instability of investment and the fluctuations in the importing power of exports.[1]

This is not to say that particular underdeveloped countries may not seriously suffer from short-run export instability. But the generalization that the underdeveloped countries as exporters of primary products are especially vulnerable to short-run instability in the world market demand, and that this problem can be solved only by international commodity stabilization schemes, has now to be treated with great reserve. As a consequence, at the international level the focus of attention has shifted from commodity stabilization schemes to various monetary and financial schemes to compensate for short-run fluctuations on export receipts and ease the supply of international liquidity. As we shall see, these schemes to compensate

[1] For a full treatment of this subject, see A. I. MacBean, *Export Instability and Economic Development*, London 1966; see also J. D. Coppock, *International Economic Instability*, New York 1962.

short-run fluctuations in their turn tend to develop into schemes for increasing longer-run financial aid to the underdeveloped countries.

For a number of underdeveloped countries still heavily dependent on the export of a few primary products, the gains from further international specialization in export production and the risks of short-run instability may still have to be carefully weighed in the light of their individual circumstances. In many cases it may turn out that the fluctuations in their export receipts are due to fluctuations in the volume of export production which may be reduced, to some extent, by appropriate domestic policies, particularly by appropriate pricing policies of the state agricultural marketing boards. Further, the risk of short-run export instability is by no means a conclusive argument for setting up import-substituting domestic manufacturing industry. There are two other policy alternatives. First a country may try to accumulate more adequate foreign exchange reserves, adding to them when export prices are high and drawing down on them when export prices are low. In many countries, the frequent 'foreign exchange crises' attributed to export market instability have been aggravated by their tendency to invest all the available foreign exchange receipts up to the hilt in longer-term development projects instead of maintaining adequate foreign exchange reserves. Second, a country may try to diversify its range of primary exports. In the generally buoyant economic climate of the post-war years there is less danger that a decline in demand for one primary export may develop into a wholesale depression of the 1930s type affecting all primary exports. Countries such as Thailand and Malaysia have successfully diversified their exports by encouraging the production of new crops, such as maize and palm oil, to supplement the traditional exports of rice and rubber.

Long-run export pessimism

The general tendency that, as their income rises, people tend to spend a smaller proportion of their income on basic needs such as food and clothing has long been taken to support the view that the world market demand for primary exports from the underdeveloped countries would show a stagnant or a declining long-run trend. This pessimistic view was powerfully championed by Professor Nurkse in his well-known Wicksell Lectures.[1] Nurkse believed that

[1] R. Nurkse, *Patterns of World Trade and Development*, Wicksell Lectures 1959, Stockholm 1959.

during the nineteenth century, international trade functioned as a powerful engine of growth transmitting a vigorous expansion of demand for primary products from the industrial centres of Western Europe to the newly settled regions of North America and Australasia. But he argued that this nineteenth-century mechanism is no longer available to the present-day underdeveloped countries for a number of reasons, in addition to the low income elasticity of demand for primary products. For one thing, the world industrial centre has now shifted from Western Europe to the United States which with its more abundant natural resources and greater size, has a relatively lesser need to import primary products. For another there are the various trend factors, such as the change in industrial structure of the advanced countries from light industries to heavy engineering and chemical industries with a lower raw material content, the growth of synthetic substitutes for raw materials and the growing agricultural protection in the advanced countries, which all combine to depress this long-view demand for primary products. Thus he concluded that it may no longer be sensible for the underdeveloped countries to go on specializing in primary products in the face of a declining long-run trend in world market demand. Rather, they should look to the development of the domestic manufacturing sector as an alternative engine of growth to international trade.

This 'export pessimism' occupied the centre of the stage in the first United Nations Conference on Trade and Development (UNCTAD) in 1964 where it was argued that the underdeveloped countries would suffer from a 'widening foreign exchange gap' between the projected export earnings and the import requirements to sustain the accepted target rate of 5% growth in their GNP. It was argued that unless the advanced countries adopted new trade policies or increased their aid to fill this foreign exchange gap, the underdeveloped countries would not be able to achieve the 5% target rate of economic growth.[1]

The 'export pessimism' has now been proved to be unfounded. Contrary to the United Nations projections based on the export performance of the underdeveloped countries during the 1950s, the export earnings of these countries expanded rapidly during the 1960s. During that decade their export earnings increased at the rate of 6·4% a year; even those countries without major petroleum exports

[1] R. Prebisch, *Towards a New Trade Policy for Development*, New York 1964.

achieved a 6% rate of increase. They also achieved their 5% target rate of growth in GNP.[1]

The basic theoretical weakness of pessimistic projections of the world market demand for the exports from the underdeveloped countries stems from their emphasis on the concept of the income elasticity of demand and on their heavy reliance on aggregate statistical trends instead of studying the export prospects from the standpoint of each underdeveloped country. To begin with, not all primary exports have low income elasticity of demand: various 'luxury food' items, such as meat, shrimps, fruit and vegetables, have very high income elasticities of demand and the success of some of the underdeveloped countries in switching their production towards these items contributed to their export expansion during the 1960s. More importantly, from the standpoint of an individual underdeveloped country, its prospects of increasing the export of a particular product depends not so much on the income elasticity of the total world market demand, but on the *price* elasticity of the demand facing it. This depends on its share of the world market for that particular export and on the competitiveness of its price compared with those of the rival producers. Recent empirical studies have served to show that when approached in these terms there are considerable opportunities of export expansion in the underdeveloped countries. Even those which are dependent on a few major exports with a large share in the world market can shift to 'minor exports' which can add up to very substantial expansion in export receipts.[2]

The introduction of the vital factors of relative costs and prices gives a somewhat different perspective on the world market demand conditions facing the underdeveloped countries. Thus the slow rate of expansion of exports from the underdeveloped countries during the 1950s and their rapid expansion during the 1960s is generally explained in terms of the changes in the rate of growth in incomes of the advanced countries who are the chief buyers of these exports. This is true as far as it goes. But we should also take the price factors into account. After the exceptionally high prices they

[1] *Partners in Development*, the Pearson Commission Report on International Development, London 1969, ch. 2, and B. I. Cohen and D. G. Sisler, 'Exports of developing countries in the 1960s', *Review of Economics and Statistics*, November 1971.

[2] See I. Little, T. Scitovsky and M. Scott, *Industry and Trade in Some Developing Countries*, OECD 1970, ch. 7, and A. D. de Vries, *The Export Experience of Developing Countries*, IBRD 1967.

enjoyed for their primary exports during the Korean war boom, the underdeveloped countries seem to have been slower in making appropriate readjustments to their prices compared with the rival producers in the advanced countries. Thus Professor Cairncross has suggested that the slow rate of growth of the primary exports from the underdeveloped countries during the period 1950-7 was not due to the sluggish world market demand; that it was primarily due to the failure of the underdeveloped countries as a group to reduce the prices of their primary exports compared with the primary exports from the advanced countries.[1]

Arguments for protection of domestic industry

(1) One of the arguments frequently used to justify the protection of the domestic manufacturing industry in the underdeveloped countries is derived from the concept of 'disguised unemployment' in agriculture. It is argued that, although the marginal product of labour in subsistence agriculture is very low or may even be zero because of the population pressure on land, the agricultural worker nevertheless enjoys a share of the product from the family farm which is equal to his average product and much higher than his marginal product. But in order to attract this worker to the manufacturing sector, he would have to be paid wages at least equal to the real income he enjoys in the agricultural sector, and somewhat more to induce him to leave his village. Thus there is a distortion in the labour market causing the manufacturing sector to employ too little labour because it is obliged to pay wages higher than the alternative social opportunity cost of labour as measured by the marginal product of labour in agriculture. Hence, the manufacturing sector should be given protection to correct this distortion in the allocation of labour.

Now, as we have already seen in Chapter 6, the removal of surplus labour from agriculture is not socially costless even if we are prepared to assume that its marginal product is zero. The workers transferred to the manufacturing sector would consume the whole of the higher wages they receive in the manufacturing sector and this would add to the total consumption of the community and reduce savings. But leaving this consideration aside, the 'disguised unemployment' argument for protection is vitiated by a number of weaknesses.

[1] A. K. Cairncross, *Factors in Economic Development*, London 1962, pp. 200-2.

It is undoubtedly true that in most underdeveloped countries wages in the manufacturing sector are much higher than in agriculture—frequently about twice as high. But one part of the wage differential is attributable to rational economic factors such as the higher cost of living in towns compared with the rural areas and the premium which the employers in the manufacturing sector are willing to pay to retain a stable labour force which has acquired some experience and training. The other part of the wage differential which does not reflect genuine economic differences arises mainly from the artificial restrictions introduced by the greater trade union power in the urban centres and the government's own minimum wage and welfare legislation, which can be enforced only in the larger manufacturing concerns. Here, the obvious way of reducing the distortion in the labour market is to remove these artificial restrictions rather than to give a tariff protection to the manufacturing sector.

The 'disguised unemployment' argument distracts attention from these artificial distortions in the labour market. But even if we accept the proposition that, in addition to the artificial distortions, 'disguised unemployment' in subsistence agriculture further introduces a spontaneous distortion into the labour market, the appropriate method of correcting it would be to give a wage *subsidy* and not a *tariff* protection to the manufacturing sector. This follows from a general principle put forward by international trade theorists that a 'domestic distortion' should be corrected by a subsidy directed at its source within the domestic economy and not by a tariff or a tax on foreign trade.[1] The first advantage of a wage subsidy is that it specifically encourages a greater amount of labour to be employed by the manufacturing sector. In contrast, the tariff does not have this specific effect. As we have seen in Chapter 5, in spite of the high tariff protection given to them, manufacturing industries in the underdeveloped countries tend to adopt excessively capital-intensive and labour-saving methods of production—because of the government policy of granting them low interest loans and the privilege of importing capital goods cheaply at the overvalued official exchange rates. The second advantage of a wage subsidy is that it does not introduce an additional cost or distortion other than the cost of the subsidy itself. On the other hand, a tariff

[1] See H. G. Johnson, 'Optimal trade intervention in the presence of domestic distortions', reprinted in *Readings in International Trade*. Ed. J. Bhagwati, Harmondsworth 1969.

corrects the distortion in the labour market only at the cost of introducing a new distortion in foreign trade. By raising the price of imports relatively to the price of exports, it imposes a loss to the consumers and reduces the incentive for export production. The fact that the tariff on manufactured imports has the effect of turning the terms of trade against the domestic producers of agricultural exports and thereby discouraging export expansion is not always fully appreciated by the advocates of protection. Finally, it should be noted that wages form only a small part, say 10% or 15%, of the gross value added in most manufacturing industries in the underdeveloped countries. This means that even if we are willing to grant a 50% wage subsidy this is equivalent only to a tariff rate of 5% to $7\frac{1}{2}$% required to correct the distortion in the labour market. It is a far cry from this to the characteristically high tariff rate of 50% or above which is generally given to the manufacturing industries in the underdeveloped countries.[1]

(2) The second argument for protection is the 'infant industry' argument. According to this argument temporary protection should be given to a newly set up manufacturing industry during the period of 'infancy' when its costs are high because of lack of experience and various 'teething troubles'; as the industry matures through the process of 'learning-by-doing' it is able to reduce costs and withstand international competition, and then the protection should be removed. Economists have long accepted this as a logical exception to the free trade principle, merely pointing out the practical difficulties of correctly selecting the industry with a genuine prospect of lower longer-run costs and of removing the tariff when it becomes unnecessary. Recently, international trade theorists have sharpened this argument.[2] They point out that the mere fact that an industry is expected to incur losses during an initial period to be followed by profits later is not in itself a sufficient ground for giving it special encouragement. For, if the future profits were high enough to outweigh the initial losses, private enterprise would not be deterred from investing in this industry provided there is an efficient capital market to advance loans to tide over the initial losses. Special encouragement is needed only if investment in new industry yields 'external economies' or social benefits which cannot be wholly appropriated by the private investor. For example, new methods

---

[1] I. Little, T. Scitovsky and M. Scott, *Industry and Trade in Some Developing Countries*, London 1970, ch. 4.
[2] Johnson, op. cit.

of production pioneered at considerable cost by a private investor may be freely imitated by others, or a new firm having trained its labour force may lose some of its skilled workers to other firms. Interpreted in this way, the 'infant industry' argument becomes a species of 'domestic distortion'; it should be corrected by subsidies directed at the source of distortion for the encouragement of research, training and education and not by a tariff protection granted to the manufacturing industry as such.

This new formulation of the 'infant industry' argument has an interesting implication. As we have seen, the manufacturing sector in the underdeveloped countries has a ready and even a privileged access to the organized capital market whereas the agricultural sector is handicapped by the underdevelopment of the rural capital market. Further, as dramatically illustrated by the 'Green Revolution', the scope for technical innovations and the need to encourage the adoption of new techniques through the process of 'learning-by-doing' may be greater in agriculture than in manufacturing industry. Thus agriculture may have a better claim to be treated as an 'infant industry' than the manufacturing sector.

(3) The third argument for the promotion of domestic industry emphasizes the 'dynamic stimulus' and the secondary rounds of activities which manufacturing industry can generate through the 'vertical linkages' with the other sectors of the economy as contrasted with the 'static' efficiency in the allocation of resources according to the comparative costs principle. This type of argument is associated with the 'unbalanced-growth' approach put forward by Professor Hirschman.[1] We shall now show that, viewed in the context of an open economy with international trade, the 'unbalanced-growth' approach based on a mechanical concept of 'linkages' turns out to be as unsatisfactory as the 'balanced-growth' approach.

The concept of 'vertical linkages' is based on the assumption of the technically given and fixed input–output coefficients between the different sectors of the economy. Thus an expansion of output in one sector is supposed to increase the demand for the inputs from the other sectors through the 'backward' linkages: e.g. the setting up of a domestic textile industry would stimulate the expansion of locally produced raw cotton to supply the new industry. The expansion of the output in a given sector is also supposed to increase the

---

[1] A. O. Hirschman, *The Strategy of Economic Development*, New Haven 1958.

supply of input to other sectors which use its output as their input through the 'forward' linkage: e.g. the setting up of a domestic steel industry would stimulate the growth of engineering industries because of the availability of locally produced steel.

The basic weakness of this approach is that it focuses attention only on the *technically* possible linkages between the *quantities* of inputs and outputs without explicitly considering the economic realization of these linkages which depends on the *costs and prices* of the inputs and outputs. This limitation is brought out sharply in the context of international trade. It then becomes apparent that the setting up of a new industry would generate economically beneficial secondary rounds of activities through the technical linkages only if the locally produced inputs were cheaper than the imports and if it were profitable to sell the locally produced outputs to the domestic market instead of exporting them. To some extent the natural advantages of location and the higher transport costs to more distant foreign markets would help the growth of local economic activities. Beyond this, the principle of comparative advantage is as important in deciding the pattern of *vertical* international specialization between different stages of production as it is in deciding the more familiar pattern of *horizontal* international specialization between different final products.

To illustrate, consider the argument that the textile industry in an underdeveloped country should be given tariff protection on the ground that it would encourage the local production of raw cotton, If the country does not have a comparative advantage in cotton growing, then the locally grown cotton would be more expensive than the imported cotton and the textile industry would be handicapped by having to pay a higher than world market price for its raw material. Suppose that the country does have a potential comparative advantage in cotton but hitherto cotton has not been grown because of an inefficient internal transport or marketing organization. In that case, it would be more economic to subsidize directly the transport and marketing of raw cotton instead of indirectly giving tariff protection to the textile industry to create the demand for cotton. Finally, if the locally produced cotton is competitive on the world market, it would not benefit the cotton growers to sell their produce to the textile industry unless they could get the same price as they would obtain by exporting the cotton. In fact, the cotton and jute growers of Pakistan suffered from the technical linkages with the domestic textile and jute manufacturing industries since the government reduced the prices given to raw cotton and jute to below the world market prices in its attempt to encourage the expansion of manufactured cotton and jute exports.[1] Similarly, the setting up of a domestic steel industry would not encourage the growth of local engineering industries unless the locally produced steel was at least as cheap as the imported steel.

Finally, we may question the generalization that the expansion of the manufacturing sector is likely to create stronger linkages than the expansion of agriculture with the rest of the economy. If the expansion of the domestic manufacturing industry can increase the demand for locally produced raw materials, the expansion of domestic agriculture can also increase the demand for locally produced inputs, such as tools and equipment and fertilizer. The relative importance of these linkages will depend on local economic conditions and 'the comparative costs of the country. Further, the expansion of agricultural and primary exports from a country may enable it to realize the economies of scale in processing these materials instead of exporting them as raw materials. This process of 'export substitution', i.e. substituting the exports of processed or semi-manufactured materials for the exports of raw materials, has the advantage over the 'import substitution' type of industrialization in that it is not limited by the smallness of the domestic market. But it has to face the trade obstacles erected by the advanced countries in the form of 'tariff escalation', i.e. letting in the raw materials free of duty while imposing progressively higher rates of tariff duty according to the stages of processing for the processed and semi-manufactured materials. The subject of the trade obstacles created by the advanced countries will be discussed later.

Economic development through freer trade

We have seen that the various arguments in favour of economic development through domestic industrialization and import substitution do not stand up to critical scrutiny. Pessimism about the prospect of export expansion from the underdeveloped countries has proved untenable both because the aggregate volume of international trade has been expanding rapidly during the recent decades and also because individual underdeveloped countries can increase their share of the market for popular exports by reducing costs. Further, there has also been a rapid expansion of manufactured

[1] See Little, Scitovsky and Scott, op. cit., p. 70.

exports from some underdeveloped countries, notably from Taiwan, South Korea, Singapore, India, Pakistan, Mexico and Brazil.

If this is accepted, international trade still remains an important engine of growth and the argument for seeking an alternative engine of growth through domestic industrialization and internal 'balanced growth' is seriously weakened. It may well be argued that while export expansion offers the most promising path of economic development for the majority of the underdeveloped countries which are small or are endowed with suitable natural resources, an internal balanced-growth approach may be more suitable for the large, densely populated countries with meagre natural resources, such as India. Even here the argument for internal balanced growth requires to be treated with caution. It may be true that for a large country such as India internal economic development, particularly the development of the agricultural sector, may prove, in aggregate terms, to be more important than the expansion of international trade. But this is to overlook the important consideration that *at the margin*, international trade and export expansion is an important factor for development. At the margin, the choice is whether to produce the commodities which a country requires, such as food or capital goods, directly at home or acquire them indirectly through international trade in exchange for exports in which the country has a comparative advantage. Thus even a large country cannot afford to neglect the opportunities for export expansion and international trade. It is now increasingly realized that India's failure to take advantage of her opportunities to expand her exports is a serious limiting factor in her economic development.[1]

We have also seen that the main arguments for the protection of domestic industries are not arguments for imposing tariff and other restrictions on imports, but rather arguments for the correction of the distortion in the allocation of resources within the domestic economy. The 'domestic distortions' may be corrected by means of appropriate taxes and subsidies at the source of the distortions. Such a policy may also involve increasing investment in the public services, such as transport and communications, irrigation and power supply, which are important sources of external economies. But these positive measures would have to be combined with the

[1] See Manmohan Singh, *India's Export Trends and the Prospects of Self Sustained Growth*, London 1964, and B. I. Cohen, 'The international development of India and Pakistan' in *Economic Development of South Asia*, Ed. E. A. G. Robinson, London 1970.

negative measures of reducing the artificial distortions which government policy has introduced into the working of the domestic markets for factors of production and final products. Such a policy of correcting the domestic distortions, far from reducing international trade would have the effect of expanding international trade by enabling the country to realize more fully its *potential* comparative advantage in export production.

There are, however, two major obstacles in this path of economic development through freer trade, (1) the first arising from the internal difficulties within the underdeveloped countries, and (2) the second created by the external trade barriers raised by the advanced countries against the exports from the underdeveloped countries.

(1) Notwithstanding the extensive theoretical discussions on the alternative strategies of economic development the existing pattern of import-substituting domestic industrialization in most under-developed countries has largely grown up unplanned under the pressure of short-run balance-of-payments difficulties. Typically, the balance-of-payments difficulties arise from deficit financing and domestic inflation. The over-valuation of the currency at the fixed exchange rate discourages the expansion of exports while the spill-over of the excess domestic demand encourages the expansion of imports. With inadequate foreign exchange reserves this leads to foreign exchange crises and these are met by *ad hoc* attempts to cut down 'luxury' and 'inessential' imports, usually by imposing quantitative controls and import licensing. The rise in the domestic prices of these imported consumer goods stimulates the growth of the import-substituting manufacturing industries—helped by other government policies to encourage the manufacturing sector. Most of these industries are therefore not 'infant industries' with a genuine prospect of lowering costs in future. They have been set up mainly by the desire to exploit the captive domestic market catering for the 'luxury' consumption of the urban population. To begin with, the import-substitution process goes through an easy phase, taking over the ready-made local markets. But, sooner or later, it comes to a dead end, (a) because the size of the domestic market for the remaining imports gets progressively smaller in relation to the minimum efficient units of production, and (b) because of the shortage of foreign exchange to keep these industries supplied with increasing amounts of various inputs and machinery which have to be imported from abroad.

The changeover from this import-substituting policy to a policy of freer trade and export expansion involves a series of unpalatable economic reforms. First, the rate of domestic inflation has to be controlled by reducing the government budget deficit. This is made difficult both by the underdeveloped countries' inability to withstand the political pressures to increase government expenditure and their limited capacity to increase taxation. It may also be noted that if the government policy is genuinely concerned with reducing 'luxury' or 'inessential' consumption it should impose heavy taxes on these items, irrespective of whether they are imported or manufactured domestically. Next, a more flexible exchange-rate system would have to be adopted. The aim of such a system is to transmit the changes in world market prices of exports and imports in terms of local currency to the domestic producers and consumers without the excessive time lags which are inevitable under a system of fixed exchange rates combined with endemic domestic inflation. Thirdly, the prevailing system of quantitative import restrictions which give indiscriminate protection to a wide range of manufacturing industry would have to be dismantled. The liberalization of foreign trade should be combined with giving special encouragement only to those industries which have a genuine prospect of becoming internationally competitive and perhaps of even breaking out into the export markets. All these reforms are likely to encounter formidable political resistance within the underdeveloped countries. In particular, a policy of trade liberalization would have to contend with the powerful opposition from the inefficient manufacturing industries (and their labour force) from which the protection has been withdrawn.

(2) The second major obstacle in the path of the underdeveloped countries seeking economic development through freer trade is created by the various trade barriers against their exports to the advanced countries. Although the governments of the advanced countries are concerned to help the underdeveloped countries and have given substantial sums in aid, they are under considerable political pressure to protect both their domestic agricultural producers and some of their declining industries which can no longer withstand competition from the underdeveloped countries. The agricultural protection in the advanced countries affects not only the temperate zone agricultural products of some of the Latin American countries, but also some tropical products, notably sugar. South-East Asian rice producers also suffer from the protection

which Japan gives to her domestic rice producers. The declining industries in the advanced countries which stand in need of protection against the competition from the underdeveloped countries are those engaged in labour-intensive manufactures, notably textiles. Thus various types of trade barriers from conventional tariffs to quotas and 'gentlemen's agreements' have been used to restrict the export of the labour-intensive manufactures from the underdeveloped countries such as Hong Kong, Taiwan and Pakistan. Such trade restrictions are clearly against the interests not only of the producers in the underdeveloped countries but also of the consumers of these products in the advanced countries. A superior alternative would be for the advanced countries to subsidize the shift of resources out of their declining manufacturing industries in which they have lost their comparative advantage to the newer technologically more sophisticated industries where they have a comparative advantage.

In addition to these trade restrictions, the advanced countries also adopt a system of 'tariff escalation' by stages of production, discriminating against the exports of processed materials in favour of the exports of raw materials from the underdeveloped countries. We have already seen that this has a serious effect in discouraging the growth of processing industries in the underdeveloped countries. Apart from this, 'tariff escalation' tends to give the producers in the advanced countries a greater degree of 'effective' protection against the competititors from the underdeveloped countries than is apparent from the nominal rates of tariffs on the finished products. This can be illustrated by a very simple arithmetical example. Suppose that raw materials form 50% of the total value of a manufactured product in an advanced country, and suppose that the final product is given a 10% nominal tariff while the raw materials are permitted to be imported free of tariff. The value added in the advanced country is only half the total value of the finished product and thus a 10% nominal tariff on it gives the producers an 'effective' tariff rate of 20%. Professor Balassa has made calculations showing that the advanced countries do impose especially heavy barriers on the manufactured exports from the underdeveloped countries. The theory of effective protection also suggests that the trade preference for the underdeveloped countries advocated by UNCTAD may well have very substantial effects in shifting industrial production towards the underdeveloped countries.[1]

[1] B. Balassa, 'Tariff protection in industrial countries: an evaluation', *Journal of Political Economy*, December 1965. See also H. G. Johnson, *Economic*

Finally, we may briefly touch on the role of direct private foreign investment in shaping the future pattern of international trade between the advanced and the underdeveloped countries. In pursuit of their import-substitution policies, the governments of many underdeveloped countries have offered tax concessions and tariff protection to foreign manufacturing corporations to induce them to open branch factories in their territories. But so long as foreign manufacturing enterprises were orientated towards the exploitation of the protected domestic markets of the underdeveloped countries, they did not greatly contribute to the economic development of these countries. Recently, however, there has been a new departure. Many multi-national corporations now find it profitable to locate certain stages of their production in the underdeveloped countries such as Taiwan, Hong Kong, Singapore and Mexico, to take advantage of their abundant and easily trainable local labour supply to manufacture 'components' in sophisticated engineering and electronic industries which are then exported to the parent companies. This is a new development which provides a promising way of combining the capital and advanced technology of the advanced countries with the labour supply of the underdeveloped countries. Further, the underdeveloped countries can now achieve an expansion of employment in exporting industries without having to face the difficult problem of marketing the manufactured export products; the internal transactions between the different branches of a multi-national firm would serve to minimize the various trade obstacles between the countries. Yet there seems to be considerable hostility towards private foreign investment by the multi-national firms both in the receiving countries and in the investing countries. The receiving countries feel that the 'centres of decision-making' have been taken out of their control while the trade unions of the investing countries, particularly in the United States, complain about the loss of employment opportunities at home because of the 'runaway plants'.[1]

Policies Towards Less Developed Countries, The Brookings Institution, Washington, 1967, chs. III and VI for a very thoroughgoing treatment of the subject.

[1] See G. K. Helleiner, 'Manufactured exports from less developed countries and multi-national firms', *Economic Journal*, March 1973.

CONCLUSIONS:

GENERAL ISSUES OF DEVELOPMENT POLICY

In this book I have set out to provide a balanced picture of the different types of underdeveloped country at different stages of development, and a systematic examination of the arguments behind the leading economic development policies of the post-war period.

Chapters 3, 4 and 5 cover the first part of my programme. In these chapters I have provided alternatives to the conventional model of an overpopulated country at a somewhat advanced stage of general development by focusing attention on the underdeveloped countries not suffering from population pressure and at earlier stages of general development. I was also concerned with the subjective problem of discontent as distinct from the problem of material poverty, and have analysed the process of export expansion in different settings in order to appraise the prevailing reaction against the 'colonial' or 'the nineteenth-century pattern' of economic development. The problems of 'dualistic' economic structure which I have outlined are of course not peculiar to the thinly populated underdeveloped countries. They are equally present in the over-populated countries, and are frequently aggravated by population pressure. Further, all underdeveloped countries, irrespective of population pressure on national resources, have tried to encourage domestic industrialization by subsidizing the larger enterprises in the modern manufacturing sector at the expense of peasant producers and small economic units in the traditional sector. This has created a new element of 'dualism' in all these countries.

From Chapter 6 onwards I was concerned with the second part of my programme. This has led me into a critical survey of the leading ideas behind the post-war policies of economic development, such as 'disguised unemployment', the overall capital–output ratio, the critical minimum size of the development programme and the various versions of the balanced-growth theory. I have tried to show that frequently these ideas are extensions of the Keynesian and the post-Keynesian theoretical approach inappropriate to the underdeveloped countries. What I have done in effect was to bring to bear upon these modern ideas some of the relevant parts of the classical and neo-classical approach. For example, I have tried to show the weakness of the concept of a stable overall capital–output ratio in the light of the Ricardian theory. I have indicated the weakness of the balanced-growth theory based on the income effect and set patterns of expansion in consumption and production in the light of the substitution effect and flexible patterns of consumption and production of the neo-classical analysis. I have tried in particular to show that when all has been said and done about the economies of scale, indivisibilities and complementarities, we cannot ultimately afford to ignore the problem of choice, for, beyond a certain point, different lines of economic development activity compete for the available scarce resources.

In Chapter 9, I have tried to show that the prospect of economic development through freer international trade is more promising for the underdeveloped countries than has been generally believed. The chapter brings out the limitations of the assumption of the closed economy which pervades much of the theorizing on economic development, and considers the traditional reactions against foreign trade and investment in the light of current developments.

In this concluding section I shall bring out the implications of my analysis for some of the more general issues of development policy.

Dilemmas of development policy

The conventional aim of development policy is to raise the level of per capita incomes of the underdeveloped countries. But it should by now be clear that it is not sufficient merely to state this aim without squarely facing some of the painful choices between alternative goals of economic policy.

(1) First, there is the problem of choice between economic equality and economic growth. Economic equality may be pursued for its own sake, irrespective of its effect on growth. Where wealth and income are distributed very unequally and the rich are not making effective use of their income for productive purposes, it

may be possible to promote both greater equality and growth by reforms to reduce inequalities. Further, as we have seen, government policies to promote domestic industrialization may aggravate the 'economic dualism' between the bigger economic units and the better paid urban workers in the modern manufacturing sector on the one hand and the peasant producers, the small handicraft industries and rural workers in the traditional sector on the other. Here the reduction of economic dualism would promote both greater economic equality and a more efficient allocation of resources. But frequently there may be a genuine conflict between economic equality and economic growth. This may operate over a wide range of situations from the removal of surplus labour from land and the consolidation of holdings for the sake of efficient farming to the provision of higher rewards to people with higher ability and skills.

(2) Next, closely related to the first is the problem of choice between a higher level of consumption at present and a higher rate of growth in income in the future. Other things being equal, the higher the target rate of growth set for future growth, the greater the sacrifice in the lower rate of increase in consumption and/or the longer period before the fruits of economic development are available. But 'other things' are not equal. Increasing present sacrifice or prolonging the waiting period would increase hardships and would tend to intensify, rather than ease, the subjective problem of discontent and the revolution of rising expectations. Further, we come up against the crucial question of how far the existing institutional and economic framework of a developing country is capable of absorbing and investing the extra savings productively. Even leaving this question on one side, there is one further question to clear up. We may interpret the significance of raising the per capita income level in two different ways: first, we may be concerned with raising the *absolute* level of income to help the mass of the people of the underdeveloped countries to attain a certain minimum standard of living in material terms, in terms of food, clothing, shelter, health and nutrition and to raise the minimum over time; second, we may be concerned with the *relative* gap between the per capita incomes of the developed and the underdeveloped countries. A conflict between the two aims may arise if the government of an underdeveloped country is concerned more with the problem of 'catching up' with the rich countries by forced saving to finance crash programmes of investment than with the

problem of enabling a larger number of people to attain certain minimum material standards of living.

(3) Thirdly, there is the choice between higher income and economic security and independence. This problem has faced the people of the underdeveloped countries since the early stages of transition from the subsistence economy to the exchange economy as they became progressively involved in a network of economic interdependence through international trade and investment. The politicians of the underdeveloped countries frequently talk about maintaining 'economic independence' to match the political independence of their countries. If by this they mean a desire to insulate their countries against the disturbing world market forces, this would involve sacrificing not only the immediate gains to be reaped through freer international trade but also the longer-run potentialities of economic development through the adoption of the new ideas, new commodities, new methods of production and organization from the outside world. As we have seen, the underdeveloped countries' vulnerability to the short-run fluctuations in the world market demand for primary exports seems to have been exaggerated. Contrariwise, it may be argued that the underdeveloped countries with their underdeveloped internal economic framework, with their imperfect internal transport and communications and with their fragile market and administrative organization are highly vulnerable to internal disturbances brought about by unfavourable weather, national calamities and political instability. Thus the opportunity to draw upon external sources of supply of food and other vital necessities either through international trade or aid may provide a stabilizing factor. By maintaining 'economic independence' the politicians from the underdeveloped countries may also mean keeping out private foreign investment. As we have seen, the operations of multi-national corporations locating certain stages in their production in the underdeveloped countries or setting up complete industries to take advantage of the local labour supply for the export market may offer a very promising way of increasing the underdeveloped countries' participation in industrial exports. But, on the other hand, it is in this area that the underdeveloped countries are particularly sensitive to the possibility that these large powerful foreign corporations might interfere with the internal politics of their host countries.

(4) Finally, there is the problem of choice for the mass of people in the underdeveloped countries between having higher material

incomes and a faster rate of growth and preserving their traditional social, cultural and religious values and ways of life.   Here, the type of psychology attributed to them by Western writers has undergone an amusing change.   In the old days, the people of the underdeveloped countries were supposed not to respond to economic incentives and prospects of material improvement.   This was the basis of the theory of the backward-bending supply curve of labour and the policy of using negative coercive measures instead of positive economic incentives for increasing the supply of labour to the mines and plantations.   Nowadays, the people of the underdeveloped countries are supposed to be pressing forward to raise their material income level at any cost.   The new picture seems to be as much a caricature as the old one.   Anyone would wish to raise his income if this involved no cost, and the people of the underdeveloped countries are no exception to this.   The real question is how far they are willing to change their ways of life, values and attitudes towards matters such as work, saving or size of family in order to enjoy a higher material level of income.

Market mechanism and economic development

Many complex issues of development policy are raised by the question of the relative roles of the market mechanism and state action in economic development.   Without attempting to go exhaustively into this great debate, I shall consider some of its salient points.

There is a widespread and influential belief that the underdeveloped countries should rely less on the automatic market forces and more on deliberate state action to promote economic development.   This belief arises from at least three distinct sources.

First, there are the theories of the 'big push' and the 'vicious circles' which we have considered in Chapter 7.   Those who subscribe to these theories maintain that while the market mechanism can deal with small piece-meal changes, it is too weak to bring about the large concerted 'critical minimum effort' required to overcome the indivisibilities and the vicious circles.   The earlier simplistic views about the vicious circle and the low-level equilibrium trap have however become increasingly implausible in the light of the experiences during the last two decades during which the underdeveloped countries have shown a fairly high average rate of growth in GNP, about 5% per annum, and this rate of growth appears to have taken place in a series of small continuous steps instead of by discontinuous jumps.

Second, the distrust of the market forces in many underdeveloped countries arises not so much from considerations of economic growth as from considerations of economic equality and security. It is believed that the free play of the market forces would exaggerate economic inequalities and lead to foreign economic domination in the context of international trade and foreign investment. This is closely related to the choice between alternative goals of policy which we have outlined in the previous section. It is for the government and the people of each underdeveloped country to decide how far they are willing to sacrifice the conventional goal of increasing per capita incomes to satisfy the alternative goals. Having decided on a consistent set of ends, it is possible to look upon the market mechanism and state action as the means of achieving these ends and to try to strike a balance between the two according to their comparative efficiency in achieving the given goals.

Third, at a semi-popular level, the antipathy towards the market mechanism arises from an ideological identification of the use of the market mechanism as 'laissez-faire' and the use of the government administrative machinery as 'planning'. It is necessary to clarify a number of points here.

To begin with, the conventional view of market mechanism versus planning obscures the fact that in most underdeveloped countries the development of the market economy and the capacity of the government to exercise control over the economic system go hand in hand. Thus in an underdeveloped country where the larger part of the resources is still engaged in subsistence production, even the most planning-minded government must start by encouraging the development of an exchange economy as the chief method of mobilizing the resources of the subsistence economy. As we have seen in Chapter 2, the traditional method of promoting the growth of the market economy has been the provision of better transport and communications and law and order to stimulate the expansion of exports and increase of government revenue from taxes on foreign trade. The government's capacity to exercise control over the economy can be pictured as a continuing process. The spread of the exchange economy from the foreign trade sector to the rest of the domestic economy would serve to widen the government's tax base while the gradual development of a domestic capital market

and financial institutions would enable the government to supplement its taxation capacity by internal borrowing. In this perspective,
the development of the market economy and the government's
capacity to plan and control the economy are complementary. The
success of development planning may be judged, not only by its
direct measurable effects on output but also by its indirect effects in
building up or destroying economic institutions which affect the
future productive capacity of the country.

Next, the deliberate use of the market mechanism to achieve the
given goals of economic policy can be distinguished from the *laissez-
faire* policy of non-interference with the market forces.   The use
of the market mechanism as an instrument of economic policy
involves (1) taxes and subsidies to influence the free market pattern
of resource allocation between different industries to correct 'distortions' or to take account of 'external economies'; (2) fiscal and
monetary policies to influence the aggregate level of consumption
and investment. This *indirect* method of planning or trying to achieve
policy goals through the use of market mechanism should, however,
be sharply distinguished from the *direct* method of planning using
the administrative machinery of the government. The economic
development plans of the underdeveloped countries are usually
formulated in terms of the target figures of investment and production planned for the public and private sectors. But they do not
always indicate by what mechanisms these plans are to be carried out.
In some countries, the private sector may be induced to carry out
its part of the plan, mainly by the market incentives or disincentives.
In others, the private sector may be subject to detailed administrative
planning at every stage of its decision-making, such as the amount
of foreign exchange it can get, the type of goods it can import and
the type of investment it can undertake.

The common experience in the underdeveloped countries is that
compared with the indirect method of planning using the market
mechanism, the direct bureaucratic planning by the government is a
very cumbrous and inefficient method of rationing scarce resources
and coordinating the plans of different sectors of the economy.
Beyond a certain point the difficulties and delays in coordinating
the different types of direct controls tend to paralyze economic
activity, even in countries with a well-developed administrative
system. Thus most countries have to fall back increasingly on
'indicative planning' based on the decentralized decision-making

process through the market mechanism—with appropriate corrections.[1]

Finally, we may briefly touch upon the problem of striking a balance between state enterprise and private enterprise. In most underdeveloped countries, state enterprises operate not only in the traditional sphere of social overhead capital, such as transport and communications, power supply and irrigation, but also in ordinary manufacturing industry. Frequently state enterprises are run less efficiently than private concerns and show lower rates of return on the capital invested. This is sometimes defended on the ground that state enterprises are not concerned with profit-making but have to take into account other social goals. Now state enterprises may show lower returns or actual losses for two distinct reasons. (1) Sometimes the losses may stem from wrong pricing policies. Thus, prices charged for public transport tend to remain sticky in spite of rising costs created by domestic inflation, and the government may be unable to raise the prices to economic levels for fear of public protests. (2) At other times, the losses arise directly from sheer inefficiency or from the wrong choice of projects influenced by considerations of national prestige rather than by economic considerations. Theoretically, it can be argued that since the government should take a long-term view of gains and losses than private enterprise, it should take bigger risks and try to fill in the gaps left by private enterprise; and that a pioneering lead by the government is especially needed in the early stages of economic development when the private entrepreneurs would lack the knowledge and resources to venture into new risky lines of investment. But in practice, the expansion of the public sector in some underdeveloped countries frequently takes the opposite pattern of nationalizing or taking over the concerns which have already been successfully operated by private enterprise.

Education and investment in human capital

A popular argument for extending the public sector and direct state action for economic development is that there is a shortage of private entrepreneurs in the underdeveloped countries. This overlooks the fact that, in order to have successful economic development by direct state action, the same scarce entrepreneurial qualities

[1] See G. Myrdal, *Asian Drama*, London 1968, vol. II, chs. 19 and 20, for a critique of Indian planning. See also I. Little, T. Scitovsky and M. Scott, *Trade and Industry in Some Developing Countries*, London 1970, chs. 6 and 9.

are needed in the public sector also, and that there is a general shortage of entrepreneurs and managers in both sectors. The administrative machinery in most underdeveloped countries is notoriously weak, and to extend the public sector is to overburden their civil servants with a horde of new entrepreneurial and managerial functions before they are effectively able to fulfil their basic administrative functions such as the maintenance of law and order, the provision of essential public services and the collection of taxes.

It is now increasingly recognized that many underdeveloped countries may be held back, not so much by a shortage of savings as by a shortage of skills and knowledge resulting in the limited capacity of their organizational framework to absorb capital in productive investment. Thus, attention has shifted from capital to education, from investment in material capital to investment in human capital. This is a great advance on the older approach of trying to mobilize the brawn-power rather than the brain-power of the people of the underdeveloped countries as illustrated by the theory of 'disguised unemployment'. But even the new approach has not fully faced up to the difficult problem of raising the level of skills in the underdeveloped countries.

First, it is too readily assumed that the problem can be solved by breaking the bottlenecks on the supply side. If there are too many lawyers and too few engineers, for example, then it is thought that this can be cured by opening more engineering colleges. This ignores the vital role which salary differentials (combined with prestige and security) play in allocating skilled manpower into different occupations. There are too many lawyers and too few engineers in some underdeveloped countries because lawyers earn more than engineers. The opening of more engineering colleges without upgrading the rewards from engineering will not increase the members of that profession. This is one of the instances where the indirect method of stimulating development through the manipulation of the market mechanism is likely to be very effective. In a moment we shall see the reasons why the overcrowded learned professions of the underdeveloped countries should be so responsive to demand factors.

Secondly, it is too readily assumed that the specific types of skills required for development can be foreseen in advance so that educational expansion can take place by supplying the correct number of 'missing components' of various types which can be neatly fitted into a given framework. This approach works well enough in the earlier stages of educational expansion immediately after political independence, where there are unfilled vacancies and obvious gaps left by the departing expatriates. But just as the expansion of manufacturing industry through import-substitution has a limit, there is a limit to educational expansion through the process of job redistribution. Beyond this point the creation of new jobs to absorb the expanding numbers of graduates from schools and universities becomes more important. Now the rate at which a developing country can absorb the new supply of trained people is basically limited by its general rate of economic growth. But in order to accelerate economic growth, the existing supply of trained people must be capable of providing dynamic leadership: this may take the form of improvements and radical adaptations in the administrative and organizational framework, increasing its capacity to absorb capital for development; or it may take the form of technical innovations, research and new applications of existing knowledge to local problems. In either case, it becomes more important to increase the supply of more qualified administrators, entrepreneurs, and general scientists rather than to increase the specific type of people who can be fitted as missing components into a given framework. It is more difficult to increase the supply of administrators, entrepreneurs and general scientists, since their basic function is to change the economic organization of the country in more productive directions instead of being fitted into a given framework.

This distinction is also important in assessing the value of foreign technical experts to the developing country. They are most useful where there is a definite niche in the organization of a developing country into which they can be fitted. But once they go beyond the function of being missing components, to try to become dynamic agents of change within the government framework, they are likely to meet with less success. For this, the knowledge of local conditions is more important than just general 'technical know-how', and foreign experts generally do not stay long enough in a country to acquire it. At the other extreme, foreign teachers may be able to perform the very valuable function of transmitting the general scientific methods and approaches to problems.

The last weakness of the 'investment in human capital' approach is that it tends to think too much in terms of applying *material* resources, such as providing more educational buildings and equipment, to increase human capital. This ignores the fact that in most developing countries the really serious limitation to the formation of new human capital is the meagre initial supply of human capital, in the form of limited numbers of qualified people. The various alternative uses of these very scarce human resources give rise to much the hardest problems of choice: first, between using them in directly productive occupations or in the teaching profession for further capital formation; and second, between various ways of using a given teaching capacity, which leads us to the thorny problems of the educational policy for economic development.

If it is accepted that economic development requires a class of exceptionally able people with high qualifications to provide the dynamic leadership, then the appropriate policy would be to restrict the number of students to that which can be effectively taught with the existing numbers of teachers and to give them intensive training according to their ability. This is the educational equivalent of 'tightening the belt' for those who are not accepted and using 'capital-intensive' techniques in human terms for those who are accepted. But in most developing countries powerful forces are working in the opposite direction. The governments are faced with popular demands for equal educational opportunities, not only between the rich and the poor which do not conflict with selection according to ability, but also between the more gifted and less gifted students. These demands can be met only by spreading the existing teaching capacity so thinly over everyone that it becomes ineffective.

What has happened in many developing countries, particularly in Asia, is that the governments have embarked on 'crash programmes' of educational expansion well beyond the capacity of the limited number of teachers. When these badly taught children finish their secondary school, they can find few opportunities for employment or apprentice training as in the advanced countries. Thus, a much larger proportion seek entry into universities and other institutions of higher education which are in their turn suffering from acute shortage of teaching staff. The general lowering of academic standards which follows tends to lower the efficiency of the graduates employed both in the private and the public sector, and does not promise well for the formation of a dynamic leadership for economic development. What is more tragic, the high quality human resources which could have provided such a leadership remain imperfectly mobilized or wasted through the overcrowding of the educational institutions and the impossibility of giving selective teaching and attention to the more gifted students. This also means that fewer students are qualified for study abroad. In recent years the number of scholarships offered by advanced countries on both sides of the Iron Curtain has outstripped the supply of suitable students from the underdeveloped countries, and this in spite of the vast reservoir of human ability which remains locked within the overcrowded educational systems of these countries.

Whatever the idealistic reasons for which the governments of the developing countries embarked on 'crash' educational programmes, the real driving force behind the popular demand for education on the part of the students and their parents is the desire to obtain good jobs afterwards. The image which inspires them is still that of the educated elite enjoying a standard of living many times higher than the per capita income level of their country. This is in fact the most important way in which 'the revolution of rising expectations' works among the educated classes of the developing countries. Few governments have been able to resist its pressure and follow a more selective and functional educational policy which might promote economic development. Yet few countries can go on absorbing poorly trained university graduates at a faster rate than their general economic growth. Sooner or later, with their present pattern of educational expansion, many developing countries will have to contend with one of the most explosive problems of discontent and frustration: that of graduate unemployment.

International aid

Much of the writing on the underdeveloped countries is concerned with the argument for increasing international aid to these countries. In this book, I have set myself a different aim—to study the economics of the underdeveloped countries as an academic discipline by examining the logical and factual basis of the various theories and policies of economic development which have been put forward. I have done this for two reasons: (1) while an aid-oriented approach is bound to look upon the central problem of economic development in terms of increasing the amount of resources available to the underdeveloped countries, I believe that the more important problem may frequently be the problem of increasing the efficiency of the use of these resources; (2) while an aid-oriented approach emphasizes what the advanced countries should do to help the underdeveloped countries by improving the external trade and aid opportunities available to these countries, I believe that frequently these countries have not been able to take full advantage of the existing external opportunities because of their inappropriate internal economic policies which only they can change. Thus, while there is considerable scope for the advanced countries to help the under-developed countries, particularly by removing the various trade obstacles to the exports from the underdeveloped countries, the conventional preoccupation with the problem of increasing inter-national aid to the underdeveloped countries frequently distracts attention from some of the more important problems of economic development.

The volume of international aid to the underdeveloped countries increased rapidly during the late 1950s. By 1960, the net flow of official aid from the OECD countries of Western Europe, North America, Japan and Australia reached $4·7 billion and increased to $5·9 billion in 1965. Since then the increase in official aid has been less rapid. Recently some of the rich oil-exporting countries have joined the ranks of the aid donors. Thus in 1975, the total net flow of development assistance was $19·1 billion consisting of $13·6 billion from the OECD countries and $5·5 billion from the OPEC coun-tries. These figures however show disbursements from the donor countries for all purposes, including technical assistance and contri-butions to the international institutions which carry out multilateral lending on a commercial basis. If we reclassify the medium and long-term capital inflows to the underdeveloped countries on the basis of their concessional element, in 1970, we have $2·1 billion of official grants, $2·4 billion of concessional loans and $6 billion of loans at market terms, making up a total net flow of capital of $10·5 billion. In 1975, the official grants were $6 billion, the concessional loans $7·6 billion, and loans at market terms $25·1 billion making up a total net flow of $38·8 billion (in current US dollars).[1]

The need to increase the official aid on concessional terms to the underdeveloped countries has been the perennial theme of the 'North–South Dialogue' since the 1950s. The United Nations launched its successive Development Decades by setting up an aid target of not less than 1% of the donor countries' GNPs (in 1975 the official aid flow amounted to 0·36% of the donors' GNP). The Pearson Commission Report, a major essay in persuasion to increase aid, bewailed 'the crisis in aid'.[2] The successive UNCTADs

[1] World Development Report 1978, Text Tables 22 and 29 and Development Assistance, 1971, OECD, Paris 1971.
[2] Partners in Development, The Pearson Commission Report on International Development, London 1969.

introduced a variety of schemes for increasing aid either directly or by changing the terms of trade in favour of the underdeveloped countries.

The weakness of the conventional arguments for aid is that they straddle uneasily between the 'economic' argument emphasizing the productivity of aid and the 'moral' argument emphasizing the need to relieve the material poverty of the people in the underdeveloped countries, mixed with appeals to the political and economic self-interests of the aid-giving countries. The economic argument is based on the presumption that there are abundant opportunities for employing capital productively in the underdeveloped countries which cannot be adequately met by ordinary loans on commercial terms from the World Bank or by private investment. But considerable doubts have been cast on this presumption through the wasteful use of aid funds, and it is increasingly recognized that in many countries the real limitation may be set by the capacity to invest rather than by a shortage of investible resources. Even the Pearson Report has to admit that 'the correlation between the amounts of aid received in the past decades and the growth performance is very weak' (p. 49).

A striking feature in the pattern of capital flows to the underdeveloped countries during the 1960s was the growth of private investment and of loans on market terms. Direct Foreign Investment which was a trickle during the 1950s accelerated during the 1960s. Initially the most important sectors were primary products and import-substituting manufacturing. But in recent times, investment for export-oriented manufacturing production has also started to grow. As we have seen, by 1970, the capital inflows at market terms to the underdeveloped countries was $6 billion, exceeding the total official grants and concessional loans of $4·5 billion. By 1975, the loans at market terms grew to $25·1 billion compared with $13 billion of official aid. But the distribution of the different types of capital flows to the two broad categories of underdeveloped countries is also striking. Thus during the 1970–5 period, about 70% of the net capital flows into the Low Income Countries consisted of official aid and only about 30% of the capital flows was obtained on commercial terms. For the Middle Income Countries, the proportions were reversed. They obtained over 70% of their capital flows from private investment and from loans on market terms.[1]

[1] *World Development Report 1978*, Text Table 30.

The fact that the Low Income Countries can borrow only a limited amount of capital on commercial terms has been used as an argument for giving them more official aid on concessional terms. But in order to make the 'economic' argument for aid convincing, it is still necessary to show not merely that they are in greater need of aid because of their lower per capita incomes but also that they have a sufficient capacity, in terms of effective domestic economic management, to absorb greater quantities of outside capital flows and use them productively. It is at this point that the argument for aid tends to shift from the productivity criterion to the need criterion and from the 'economic' to the 'moral' argument for increasing aid. But even if we are willing to accept the moral judgment that the concept of the Welfare State within a nation should be extended internationally, it does not necessarily lead to an argument for giving *capital aid for* development purposes. For it is possible to argue that a more economic way of reducing inequalities in international income distribution is to allocate the world capital resources wherever they yield the highest returns and then distribute the resultant product as grants in the form of *final consumers' goods*, directed not simply towards the poor countries but to the poorer sections of the population in the poor countries. Such a thoroughgoing application of the Welfare State principle in the form of *consumption aid* is not likely to be acceptable either to the aid-giving or to the aid-receiving countries. The governments of the rich countries are clearly unwilling to accept the permanent burden of giving consumption aid while the governments of the underdeveloped countries would regard such transfers of income as 'charity'.

This is not to deny the existence of a genuine and widespread desire to help the poor of the underdeveloped countries among the people of the advanced countries in their private and individual capacity. But when this moral concern is institutionalized into development aid, it has to go through the double filter of the government of the aid-giving country and the government of the aid-receiving country, each pursuing its own political and economic interests. Frequently the resultant transfer of resources may have little to do with economic development as measured in terms of the growth in aggregate GNP. It may have even less to do with the moral concern with raising the material standards of living of the poorer section of the population of the underdeveloped countries. On top of this, much confusion has been created by the advocates of aid bent on putting forward persuasive arguments for aid.

Instead of clearly stating their altruistic principle that the aim of economic aid should be only to help the developing countries, and that the richer countries should be prepared to face the considerable cost of aid-giving without expecting anything in return, they have tried to make their case more persuasive by appealing to the national self-interest of the aid-giving countries.   It then becomes increasingly difficult to distinguish the 'crypto-philanthropists' who hide altruism under the mask of national self-interest from the 'neo-colonialists' who may hide national self-interest under the mask of altruism.

The first UNCTAD meeting of 1964 which recognized the increasing stringency in official aid-giving introduced a new dimension into the argument by focusing attention on the need to expand the export earnings of the underdeveloped countries, amongst other things, by removing the trade barriers which the advanced countries have erected against the exports from the underdeveloped countries. But as we have seen, the advanced countries have been unwilling to make the painful adjustments in their trade regulations in the face of politically powerful opposition by domestic vested interests, and have been tempted to take the easier course of offering aid instead of trade. Similarly the underdeveloped countries, unwilling to make painful adjustments in their domestic economic policies, have also been tempted to seek aid to bolster their existing inefficient import-substituting industries rather than make a greater effort to expand exports. Thus the initial impact of UNCTAD towards a greater liberalization of international trade has become increasingly overlaid with the demand for more aid on various grounds. Thus the proposals for compensatory financing from the IMF and the World Bank to counteract short-run fluctuations in export receipts seem to have developed into a method of increasing long-term aid. The main outcome of the 3rd UNCTAD was the proposal to link the Special Drawing Rights in the IMF, originally introduced to increase international liquidity, with development assistance to the underdeveloped countries.

Currently, following the 4th UNCTAD, the central theme of the 'North–South Dialogue' is the demand of the underdeveloped countries for a New International Economic Order. Amongst other things, this contains two sets of proposals intended to favour the export interests of the underdeveloped countries. First, there is the proposal to set up a common fund of $3 billion as a ready source of financing buffer stocks and encouraging individual commodity agreements covering some ten to eighteen 'core' commodities of special interest to the underdeveloped countries. This has been called the 'Integrated Programme for Commodities'. Second, there is the proposal to extend the tariff preferences to the manufactured exports from the underdeveloped countries on a non-reciprocal basis. This is to be done by allowing the manufactured exports from the underdeveloped countries duty free into the markets of the developed countries while these countries would charge the going rate of tariff on similar competitive exports from the other developed countries. Thus the margin of preferences which the underdeveloped countries would receive is equal to the tariff level for those products prevailing among the developed countries under the most-favoured-nation rule of the GATT. This method of giving special preference to the manufactured exports from the underdeveloped countries has come to be known as the 'Generalized System of Preferences', the intention being that identical treatment should be applied by all the developed countries to the manufactured exports from all the underdeveloped countries.

In so far as the 'Integrated Programme for Commodities' is intended as a method of reducing the short-run instability of export earnings of the underdeveloped countries, it is likely to be ineffective and uneconomical. As we have seen in Chapter 9, price stabilization schemes based on buffer stocks and commodities are likely to destabilize the total export earnings (i.e., prices multiplied by quantities) when the fluctuations arise from the variations in the quantities of output originating in the supply conditions of the export countries rather than from the variations of the world market demand. Further, the aim of reducing instability in export earnings can be more economically achieved without locking up real resources in buffer stocks, by financial and fiscal methods such as the extension of the IMF compensatory Finance Facility or by appropriate adjustments of export taxes and subsidies in the producing countries. But the sponsors of the 'Integrated Programme for Commodities' would like to use it not only as a method of reducing short-run instability in export earnings but also as a method of transferring resources from the advanced to the underdeveloped countries, by fixing more favourable terms of trade for primary products. But this further longer-run objective can be achieved only by restricting output or by the buffer stocks purchasing commodity surpluses at prices above the longer-run equilibrium prices. The transfer of resources is supposed to take place either by making the consumers in the advanced countries pay higher prices or by making the governments of the advanced countries contribute to the financing of excessive accumulation of buffer stocks. Even if this were politically feasible, it is subject to a number of objections. First, some of the advanced countries who are themselves significant exporters of some of the commodities included in the scheme would benefit from the restriction in supply. Further, the consumers in the underdeveloped countries who happen not to be the producers of these selected commodities would suffer. On top of all this, commodity restriction schemes tend to have an adverse effect on productivity by preventing new low-cost producers from entering into the market. In so far as these potential producers are from other underdeveloped countries these countries would suffer from being deprived of the opportunity of diversifying their, exports into new commodities.

There can be no question that the underdeveloped countries would greatly benefit from the removal of the various trade barriers which have been erected against their manufactured exports in the developed countries. What can be questioned is whether the underdeveloped countries can more effectively achieve this important goal by seeking to extend the Generalized system of Preferences (GSP) under the auspices of UNCTAD or by entering into tariff-cutting negotiations on a reciprocal most-favoured-nations basis (MFN) under the auspices of the General Agreement on Tariffs and Trade (GATT). The scope for increasing the underdeveloped countries' manufactured exports through the extension of the GSP does not seem to be great since the preference margin obtainable has been eroded by reciprocal tariff-cuts brought about by the Kennedy Round and by the more recent Tokyo Round. Several detailed studies of the GSP schemes have placed an upper limit on their value for increasing the exports from the underdeveloped countries of about $1 million a year—considerably less than the effect of the Kennedy Round of tariff reductions which is estimated to have added about $1 billion a year to the underdeveloped countries' exports.[1] It would seem that the underdeveloped countries can expect to expand their exports a great deal more by entering into negotiations to cut tariffs on a reciprocal MFN basis to include products which are excluded from the GSP. Further, a major advantage of the tariff reductions on the MFN basis agreed under the auspices of the GATT

[1] See M. E. Kreinin and J. M. Finger, 'A critical survey of the New International Economic Order', *Journal of World Trade Law*, November–December 1976.

is that they are likely to be permanent and not subject to quotas and quantitative restrictions. In contrast, the GSP concessions granted on a bilateral basis by individual advanced countries are temporary and are now increasingly subject to a variety of quantitative restrictions under the guise of 'gentlemen's agreements', 'voluntary' self-restraint in the interest of 'orderly marketing', etc. Indeed the under-developed countries in seeking special preferences which discriminate in favour of their exports may be unwittingly playing into the hands of the protectionist interest in the advanced countries who are not averse from making bilateral agreements to contravene the GATT rules of non-discrimination. Finally, the underlying pre-supposition behind the demand for preferential tariff concessions under the GSP is that the existing pattern of comparative advantage between the underdeveloped and the developed countries is rigid and immut-able and that the underdeveloped countries are forever destined to remain primary producers or exporters of 'simple manufactures'. However, the export experiences of some of the underdeveloped countries have seriously undermined this presupposition. Successful countries such as South Korea or Brazil have shown that by pursuing appropriate domestic economic policies oriented towards export expansion, they can become formidable competitors in the world market for a wide range of manufactured goods, including capital goods such as steel and shipbuilding, in a surprisingly short time. There is no reason why other underdeveloped countries should not follow this path, given the advantage of an abundant labour supply which can be trained and low wage costs. In a world of rapidly changing patterns of comparative advantage brought about by rapid changes in demand, resource availabilities and transmission of technologies, the old-fashioned notion of the underdeveloped countries as exporters of 'simple manufactures' has become obsolete. It is increasingly difficult to distinguish which particular type of manufactures are likely to be special export interests to them and which are not. Thus in their preoccupation with trying to secure GSP preferences for a narrow range of manufactured products of 'special' export interest to them at the present moment, the under-developed countries may be distracted from the more important task of seeking to lower the trade barriers on a wider range of manu-factured products in which they may unexpectedly find themselves having a comparative advantage in the not too distant future. It is paradoxical that a rear-guard action against a rapidly changing pattern of international division of labour should have been fought under the banner of a New International Economic Order.

SHORT GENERAL READING LIST

Argawala, A. N., and Singh, S. P. (Eds.), *The Economics of Underdevelopment* (Bombay 1958)

Bauer, P. T., *Dissent on Development* (London 1971)

Cairncross, A. K., *Factors in Economic Development* (London 1962)

Frankel, S. H., *The Economic Impact on Underdeveloped Societies* (Oxford 1953)

Hirschman, A. O., *The Strategy of Economic Development* (New Haven 1958)

Johnson, H. G., *Economic Policies Towards Less Developed Countries* (The Brookings Institution, Washington 1967)

Lewis, W. A., *The Theory of Economic Growth* (London 1959)

Little, I., Scitovsky, T., and Scott, M., *Industry and Trade in Some Developing Countries* (London 1970)

MacBean, A. I., *Export Instability and Economic Development* (London 1966)

Meier, G. M., *Leading Issues in Economic Development* (3rd ed., New York 1976)

Myint, H., *Economic Theory and the Underdeveloped Countries* (London 1971)

Nurkse, R., *Equilibrium and Growth in the World Economy*, (Cambridge, Mass. 1961)

Pearson, L. B. (Chairman), *Partners in Development*, Report of Commission on International Development (London 1969)

Reynolds, L. G., *Image and Reality in Economic Development* (New Haven, Conn. 1977)

Rostow, W. W., *The Stages of Economic Growth* (Cambridge 1960)

Sen, A. K., *Choice of Techniques* (3rd ed., Oxford 1968)

Wall, D. (Ed.), *Chicago Essays in Economic Development* (Chicago 1972)

INDEX